I0845933

DR. LAUREL JOHNSON PH.D.

Victorious in the storm

Copyright © 2023 by Dr. Laurel Johnson Ph.D.

All rights reserved. No part of this publication may be reproduced, stored or transmitted in any form or by any means, electronic, mechanical, photocopying, recording, scanning, or otherwise without written permission from the publisher. It is illegal to copy this book, post it to a website, or distribute it by any other means without permission.

First edition

This book was professionally typeset on Reedsy
Find out more at reedsy.com

To my mom, who has been my guiding light through every storm. Your unwavering love, strength, and support have inspired me to weather life's challenges with courage and resilience. This book is dedicated to you, the epitome of victory in the storm.

Contents

   1.

   2.

   3.

   4.

   5.

   6.

   7.

   8.

   9.

   10.

11.

12.

13.

Foreword

In the face of adversity, the true strength and resilience of the human spirit shine through. We are all familiar with the storms that life throws our way - the unexpected challenges, the trials that test our resolve, and the turbulent times that threaten to engulf us. It is during these tempestuous moments that we are forced to confront our deepest fears, summon our inner strength, and find the courage to press on.

"Victorious in the Storm" is a testament to the indomitable spirit that resides within each and every one of us. It is a profound exploration of the human experience, delving into the depths of despair and the heights of triumph. Through its captivating narrative and compelling characters, this book offers solace, inspiration, and a powerful reminder that victory can be found even in the midst of life's most turbulent storms.

As the reader embarks on the journey within the pages of "Victorious in the Storm," they will be introduced to a cast of characters whose lives are irrevocably altered by the storms that surround them. The storm, both literal and metaphorical, becomes a catalyst for transformation, setting in motion a series of events that will test the limits of their strength, resilience, and determination.

At the heart of this narrative is our protagonist, a figure who embodies the human capacity for growth, adaptability, and triumph. Through her unyielding spirit and unwavering resolve, she becomes a beacon of hope, guiding readers through the darkest corners of despair and showing them that there is always light at the end of the storm. Her journey serves as an inspiration, reminding us that we are not defined by the storms we face, but by how we weather them.

The power of "Victorious in the Storm" lies not only in its compelling characters, but also in its ability to resonate with readers on a deeply personal level. The storms depicted within this book mirror the storms of our own lives - the unexpected losses, shattered dreams, and moments of profound uncertainty. Through its pages, readers will find solace in the knowledge that they are not alone in their struggles, and that there is always hope on the horizon.

The author's skillful storytelling transports readers into the heart of the storm, immersing them in its fury and unpredictability. The vivid descriptions and atmospheric details bring the storm to life, evoking a visceral response that mirrors the emotions we experience when faced with our own trials. It is through this immersive experience that readers are able to forge a deep connection with the characters, understanding their pain, sharing their triumphs, and ultimately finding inspiration in their journey.

"Victorious in the Storm" is a book that defies genre conventions and transcends the boundaries of traditional storytelling. It is a tale of resilience, perseverance, and the triumph of the human spirit. It reminds us that storms, though fierce and formidable, are not insurmountable obstacles, but rather opportunities for growth and transformation.

Within these pages, readers will discover profound insights into the nature of resilience, the power of hope, and the importance of community. They will witness the strength that can be found in unity, as characters come together to weather the storm and emerge stronger than ever before. Through their collective journey, we are reminded of the strength that lies within our connections with others, and the transformative power of compassion and support.

"Victorious in the Storm" is more than just a book; it is a guiding light in times of darkness, a source of inspiration when hope seems fleeting. It is a reminder that storms are not meant to break us, but to shape us into stronger, more resilient individuals. As you embark on this literary journey, may you find solace, strength, and renewed hope in the face of whatever storms may come your way.

In closing, I am honored to present "Victorious in the Storm" to you, dear reader. May its pages serve as a source of inspiration, guiding you through your own trials and reminding you that even in the fiercest storms, victory is within reach. Embrace the storm, find your inner strength, and let the journey begin.

Introduction.

In the realm of literature, stories of triumph over adversity have always struck a resounding chord with readers. They remind us that even in the darkest of times, the human spirit has the capacity to rise above challenges and emerge victorious. "Victorious in the Storm" is one such remarkable masterpiece that embodies the very essence of resilience, strength, and the indomitable will to overcome.

From its opening pages, "Victorious in the Storm" plunges readers into a tempestuous world where the forces of chaos threaten to consume everything in their path. The storm, both metaphorical and literal, becomes a formidable backdrop against which the characters' true mettle is tested. It is in this crucible of uncertainty and turmoil that their triumphs are forged.

Written by a master storyteller, "Victorious in the Storm" weaves a tapestry of captivating narratives, richly layered characters, and vivid imagery that immerses readers in a world where adversity reigns supreme. The author's deft hand at crafting suspenseful plot twists and heart-wrenching moments of vulnerability ensures that readers are held spellbound from start to finish.

Central to the narrative is the protagonist, a figure who embodies the resilience and determination that lie within each of us. As the storm rages on, threatening to destroy everything she holds dear, she finds herself at a crossroads. Will she succumb to the overwhelming power of the storm, or will she rise above it, defying the odds and emerging victorious? It is this question that propels readers forward, urging them to accompany her on her perilous journey.

"Victorious in the Storm" is not merely a tale of triumph; it is a profound exploration of the human condition. Through the characters' struggles, the book delves into the depths of despair, the haunting echoes of loss, and the unyielding strength of hope. It reminds us that storms, whether metaphorical or real, are an inevitable part of life, and it is how we navigate through them that defines our character.

As readers delve deeper into the pages of "Victorious in the Storm," they are confronted with a myriad of emotions. They will experience the raw anguish of shattered dreams, the searing pain of heartbreak, and the unrelenting determination to rebuild what has been lost. The author's evocative prose captures these emotions with such intensity that readers cannot help but feel a profound connection to the characters and their struggles.

What sets "Victorious in the Storm" apart from other tales of triumph is its unflinching portrayal of the storm itself. The storm becomes a character in its own right, a relentless force that threatens to consume everything in its path. Through vivid descriptions and atmospheric details, the author breathes life into the storm, making it a palpable presence throughout the narrative. Its power and unpredictability mirror the challenges we face in our own lives, serving as a powerful metaphor for the trials and tribulations that test our resolve.

Beyond its captivating storytelling, "Victorious in the Storm" also offers profound insights into the nature of resilience and the human capacity for growth. As the protagonist navigates the treacherous waters of the storm, she discovers hidden reservoirs of strength within herself that she never knew existed. It is through her struggles that readers are inspired to reflect on their own resilience, to consider the depths of their own inner fortitude, and to find solace in the knowledge that victory is possible even in the most turbulent of times.

With its compelling narrative, deeply relatable characters, and thought-provoking themes, "Victorious in the Storm" has all the ingredients of a best-selling novel. It is a book that will resonate with readers from all walks of life, capturing their hearts and minds with its powerful message of hope and triumph. Through its pages, readers will come to understand that storms, in all their fury, can be weathered, and that within each of us lies the potential for victory, even in the face of the greatest adversity.

Chapter 1: Finding Forgiveness for Your History.

"Finding Forgiveness for Your History" encompasses the process of seeking and granting forgiveness for past actions, experiences, and mistakes. It involves acknowledging the impact of one's history, understanding the need for forgiveness, and actively working towards healing, self-acceptance, and personal growth. Each person carries a unique history consisting of their past actions, choices, relationships, and experiences. Sometimes, these histories include regrettable or hurtful moments that can weigh heavily on an individual's conscience. The title "Finding Forgiveness for Your History" suggests that it is possible to come to terms with one's past, make peace with it, and find a path towards forgiveness.

Forgiveness is a complex and deeply personal process. It involves acknowledging the pain, guilt, or shame associated with past actions and experiences, and making a conscious choice to let go of resentment, anger, and self-condemnation. Forgiving oneself and others is not about condoning or forgetting the past, but rather about freeing oneself from the burden of carrying that history. The process of finding forgiveness for one's history begins with self-reflection and acceptance. It requires an honest examination of one's actions, motivations, and the impact they may have had on others. It is essential to confront and take responsibility for any harm caused, acknowledging the pain and consequences resulting from past behaviors.

Self-acceptance is a crucial aspect of finding forgiveness. It involves developing compassion and understanding for oneself, recognizing that everyone makes mistakes and goes through periods of growth and change. Embracing one's imperfections and learning from past experiences can lead to self-forgiveness and a sense of personal liberation. Another crucial component of finding forgiveness for one's history is empathy and understanding towards others. This includes acknowledging that everyone has their own history, struggles, and moments of regret. Recognizing the humanity and fallibility in others can foster compassion and forgiveness, both towards oneself and others involved in one's history.

Seeking forgiveness from others is an integral part of the process. It requires humility, vulnerability, and genuine remorse. Approaching those who have been hurt by one's actions with humility and a sincere desire to make amends can open the door to healing and reconciliation. However, it is important to recognize that forgiveness from others is not guaranteed, and one must be prepared to accept the outcomes of their efforts. In some cases, forgiveness may not be possible or appropriate from the individuals directly involved. In such instances, finding forgiveness may involve seeking support from therapists, support groups, or spiritual leaders. These resources can provide guidance, perspective, and tools for navigating the complexities of forgiveness and healing.

Finding forgiveness for one's history also involves letting go of resentment and anger towards oneself and others. Holding onto these negative emotions only perpetuates pain and hinders personal growth. It may be necessary to practice techniques such as mindfulness, meditation, or journaling to process and release these emotions, allowing space for forgiveness and healing to take root. Ultimately, finding forgiveness for one's history is a transformative journey that can lead to personal growth, liberation, and a renewed sense of self. It is about acknowledging the past, taking responsibility for one's actions, seeking forgiveness from others, and cultivating self-compassion and understanding. By finding forgiveness, individuals can break free from the constraints of their history, learn from their experiences, and move forward with a sense of peace, purpose, and the potential for a more positive future.

Tips for finding forgiveness for your history.

1. **Self-reflection and Acceptance:** Take time to reflect on your past actions and experiences. Acknowledge any mistakes or regrets and accept that they are a part of your history. Embrace self-acceptance by recognizing that everyone makes mistakes and that you are capable of growth and change.

2. **Seek Understanding and Empathy:** Try to understand the reasons behind your past actions and the circumstances that may have influenced them. Practice empathy towards yourself, recognizing that you were doing the best you could

at the time. Extend empathy to others involved in your history, understanding that they too may have had their own struggles and limitations.

3. **Make Amends and Seek Forgiveness:** If possible, reach out to those you may have hurt or wronged in the past. Offer a sincere apology, take responsibility for your actions, and express genuine remorse. Be prepared for different responses, as forgiveness is a personal choice for each individual. Even if forgiveness is not granted, the act of seeking forgiveness can be a step towards your own healing.

4. **Release Resentment and Anger:** Holding onto resentment and anger towards yourself or others only prolongs the pain and hinders your ability to find forgiveness. Practice forgiveness exercises such as journaling, forgiveness meditation, or seeking therapy to process and release these negative emotions. Choose to let go of the past and focus on personal growth and healing.

5. **Practice Self-Compassion and Self-Care:** Be kind to yourself throughout the forgiveness journey. Practice self-compassion by treating yourself with understanding, patience, and forgiveness. Engage in self-care activities that promote your emotional and mental well-being, such as exercise, meditation, spending time in nature, or engaging in hobbies you enjoy.

Bbenefits of finding forgiveness for your history.

1. **Emotional Freedom:** Finding forgiveness allows you to let go of negative emotions such as guilt, shame, and anger. It frees you from the burden of carrying past mistakes, enabling you to experience emotional freedom and peace of mind.

2. **Improved Relationships:** Forgiving yourself and others can lead to improved relationships. It fosters understanding, empathy, and compassion, which can deepen connections and create a more positive and harmonious environment in your interactions with others.

3. **Enhanced Mental Health:** Forgiveness has been linked to improved mental health outcomes. Letting go of resentment and anger can reduce stress, anxiety, and depression, promoting overall psychological well-being and resilience.

4. **Personal Growth and Self-Development:** Finding forgiveness for your history provides an opportunity for personal growth and self-development. It allows you to learn from past mistakes, make positive changes, and cultivate a stronger sense of self-awareness and resilience.

5. **Increased Inner Peace and Happiness:** Forgiveness brings inner peace and a sense of liberation. By freeing yourself from the weight of past actions and experiences, you create space for joy, happiness, and a renewed sense of purpose in your life.

Functions of finding forgiveness for your history.

1. **Healing and Closure:** Forgiveness serves as a healing process, allowing wounds from the past to close and promoting emotional and psychological well-being. It provides closure to painful experiences, enabling individuals to move forward with their lives.

2. **Reconciliation:** Forgiveness can pave the way for reconciliation in relationships that have been strained or broken due to past conflicts. By seeking forgiveness and offering it to others, you open the possibility of rebuilding trust and fostering healthier connections.

3. **Self-Forgiveness:** Forgiving yourself is a crucial function of finding forgiveness for your history. It enables you to let go of self-blame, guilt, and shame, and to embrace self-compassion, self-acceptance, and personal growth.

4. **Breaking the Cycle:** Forgiveness breaks the cycle of negativity and resentment. It prevents the perpetuation of anger and pain, allowing individuals to break free from destructive patterns and create a more positive future for themselves and their relationships.

5. **Empowerment:** Finding forgiveness empowers individuals to take control of their own happiness and well-being. It shifts the focus from being a victim of the past to being an active participant in creating a brighter future. Forgiveness gives individuals the power to shape their own narratives and live authentically.

Importance of finding forgiveness for your history.

1. **Emotional Healing:** Forgiving yourself and others allows for emotional healing. It enables you to release negative emotions such as anger, resentment, and guilt, which can weigh heavily on your mental and emotional well-being. Forgiveness offers an opportunity to heal and find inner peace.

2. **Improved Relationships:** Forgiveness plays a vital role in improving relationships. By letting go of past grievances, you create space for healthier and more positive interactions. It fosters empathy, understanding, and compassion, which are essential for building and maintaining strong connections with others.

3. **Personal Growth:** Finding forgiveness for your history is a catalyst for personal growth. It allows you to reflect on your actions, learn from past mistakes, and make positive changes. Forgiveness encourages self-reflection, self-awareness, and a commitment to personal development.

4. **Release of Resentment:** Holding onto resentment is detrimental to your well-being. It can consume your thoughts, hinder your ability to trust, and create a negative mindset. Forgiveness liberates you from the burden of resentment, enabling you to move forward with a lighter heart and a more positive outlook.

5. **Freedom from the Past:** Dwelling on past mistakes or painful experiences can hinder your ability to live in the present and embrace the future. Finding forgiveness sets you

free from the grip of the past, allowing you to focus on the possibilities and opportunities that lie ahead.

Qualities that are important in the process of finding forgiveness for your history.

1. **Compassion:** Compassion is the ability to understand and empathize with oneself and others. It is essential in finding forgiveness, as it allows you to see the humanity and fallibility in yourself and those involved in your history. Cultivating compassion fosters a sense of understanding and opens the door to forgiveness.

2. **Self-Reflection:** Self-reflection is the practice of introspection and examining one's thoughts, feelings, and actions. It is crucial in finding forgiveness as it enables you to gain insight into your past behaviors, motivations, and their impact on others. Self-reflection helps you take responsibility and make amends.

3. **Humility:** Humility is recognizing and accepting one's limitations and mistakes. It plays a significant role in finding forgiveness as it allows you to approach others with humility when seeking forgiveness. Humility also fosters a sense of openness and willingness to learn and grow from past experiences.

4. **Patience:** Forgiveness is not an instant process; it takes time and patience. Patience is important in allowing yourself and others involved in your history to heal and process their emotions. It requires patience to navigate the complexities of

forgiveness, especially when forgiveness from others may not come immediately.

5. **Resilience:** Resilience is the ability to bounce back from adversity and navigate challenging situations. It is crucial in finding forgiveness as it helps you persevere through the emotional journey of healing and letting go. Resilience allows you to continue to grow and learn from your history, even in the face of setbacks.

Framework that can guide the process of finding forgiveness for your history.

1. **Acknowledge and Accept:** Begin by acknowledging your past actions, choices, and experiences. Accept that they are a part of your history, and recognize the impact they may have had on yourself and others. Embrace the need for forgiveness and commit to the journey.

2. **Reflect and Learn:** Engage in self-reflection to gain insight into your motivations, thought patterns, and behaviors. Learn from your past mistakes, understanding the lessons they have taught you and how you can grow from them. This reflection helps you take responsibility for your actions and make amends.

3. **Seek Forgiveness and Make Amends:** If possible, reach out to those you may have hurt and seek their forgiveness. Offer a sincere apology, express remorse, and take responsibility for your actions. Be prepared for different responses and respect the boundaries and choices of others.

4. **Practice Self-Forgiveness:** Forgive yourself for your past mistakes and shortcomings. Cultivate self-compassion and understanding, recognizing that you are human and capable of growth and change. Release self-blame and guilt, and focus on your personal growth and healing.

5. **Embrace Healing and Letting Go:** Engage in healing practices such as therapy, mindfulness, or journaling to process and release negative emotions. Practice forgiveness exercises that can help you let go of resentment and anger. Embrace the journey of healing and allow yourself to move forward with a sense of peace and freedom.

Techniques that can help in finding forgiveness for your history.

1. **Journaling:** Writing down your thoughts, emotions, and reflections can be a powerful tool in the forgiveness process. Journaling allows you to explore your feelings, gain clarity, and gain a deeper understanding of your history. It can also help you identify patterns, triggers, and areas where forgiveness is needed.

2. **Meditation and Mindfulness:** Engaging in mindfulness and meditation practices can assist in finding forgiveness. These techniques help you cultivate present-moment awareness, observe your thoughts and emotions without judgment, and develop a sense of compassion for yourself and others. Regular meditation practice can promote forgiveness and emotional healing.

3. **Therapy or Counseling:** Seeking professional help from therapists or counselors who specialize in forgiveness can provide guidance and support. Therapy sessions offer a safe space to explore your history, process emotions, and develop strategies for forgiveness. A trained professional can help you navigate the complexities of forgiveness and provide personalized techniques tailored to your needs.

4. **Visualization and Imagery:** Visualization techniques can be used to create a mental image of forgiveness and healing. Close your eyes and imagine yourself releasing negative emotions, letting go of past pain, and embracing forgiveness. Visualize a positive future and the growth that comes with forgiveness. This practice can help shift your mindset towards forgiveness and create a sense of emotional release.

5. **Self-Compassion Exercises:** Engage in self-compassion exercises to cultivate kindness and understanding towards yourself. Treat yourself with the same empathy and care you would offer to a close friend. Practice self-forgiveness affirmations, self-care rituals, and self-soothing techniques. By nurturing self-compassion, you create a foundation for forgiveness and personal healing.

Factors that can influence the process of finding forgiveness for your history.

1. **Personal Beliefs and Values:** Your belief system and values play a significant role in the forgiveness process. Cultural, religious, or spiritual beliefs may shape your understanding

of forgiveness and influence your willingness to seek or grant forgiveness. These factors can impact the importance and significance you attribute to forgiveness.

2. **Emotional Readiness:** The emotional readiness to forgive is an essential factor. It is crucial to give yourself time and space to process your emotions and heal before attempting forgiveness. Rushing the process or forcing forgiveness may hinder the healing journey and make forgiveness less genuine or sustainable.

3. **Support System:** The presence of a supportive network can greatly impact your ability to find forgiveness. Surrounding yourself with understanding and compassionate individuals who can provide guidance, empathy, and validation can make the forgiveness process more manageable. A support system can offer encouragement, perspective, and a safe space to share your experiences.

4. **Level of Responsibility:** The level of responsibility you take for your actions and their consequences can influence the forgiveness process. Accepting accountability and demonstrating genuine remorse can contribute to the willingness of others to forgive you. Similarly, recognizing the impact of external factors or circumstances on your actions can also play a role in finding forgiveness.

5. **Nature of the Offense:** The nature and severity of the offense or harm caused can impact the forgiveness process. Some offenses may be easier to forgive than others, depending on the level of trust broken, the emotional pain inflicted, or the duration of the harm. The complexity and

magnitude of the offense may require more time, effort, and support to find forgiveness.

Causes that may hinder the process of finding forgiveness for your history.

1. **Lack of Self-Reflection:** Without self-reflection, it is challenging to understand the underlying factors contributing to your history and the need for forgiveness. Avoiding self-reflection may prevent you from taking responsibility and addressing the root causes of your actions.

2. **Resistance to Letting Go:** Holding onto resentment, anger, or a desire for revenge can hinder the forgiveness process. Resistance to letting go of negative emotions keeps you stuck in the past and prevents you from embracing forgiveness and moving forward.

3. **Fear of Vulnerability:** Forgiveness requires vulnerability, as it involves acknowledging your mistakes and facing the pain you may have caused. Fear of vulnerability can make it difficult to seek forgiveness from others or to forgive yourself. It is essential to recognize and address these fears to progress towards forgiveness.

4. **Lack of Empathy:** A lack of empathy towards yourself or others involved in your history can hinder the forgiveness process. Without empathy, it becomes challenging to understand the impact of your actions or to extend forgiveness to others. Cultivating empathy is crucial for finding forgiveness.

5. **External Influences and Social Pressure:** External influences, such as societal norms or pressure from others, can impact the forgiveness process. Social expectations, cultural beliefs, or pressure to conform may create obstacles to forgiveness, making it challenging to find forgiveness for your history. It is important to recognize and challenge these external influences to find your own path towards forgiveness.

Advantages of Finding forgiveness for your history.

1. **Emotional Healing:** Forgiveness allows you to release negative emotions such as anger, resentment, and bitterness, leading to emotional healing and a sense of inner peace.

2. **Improved Relationships:** Forgiving others and yourself can foster healthier and more positive relationships by promoting empathy, understanding, and reconciliation.

3. **Personal Growth:** Finding forgiveness promotes personal growth by encouraging self-reflection, learning from past mistakes, and making positive changes in behavior and mindset.

4. **Reduced Stress and Anxiety:** Holding onto grudges and past hurts can create stress and anxiety. Forgiveness can alleviate these negative emotions, leading to improved mental well-being.

5. **Increased Empathy and Compassion:** Forgiveness cultivates empathy and compassion towards oneself and

others, fostering a greater understanding of human fallibility and promoting kindness and understanding.

Disadvantages to consider when finding forgiveness for your history.

1. **Difficulty in Letting Go:** Forgiveness requires letting go of negative emotions and attachments to past hurts, which can be challenging and may take time and effort.

2. **Risk of Repeating Patterns:** Without addressing the root causes of your actions and behaviors, there is a risk of repeating the same mistakes or engaging in harmful patterns in the future.

3. **Potential for Unrealistic Expectations:** Forgiveness does not guarantee immediate reconciliation or restoration of trust. It is important to manage expectations and understand that forgiveness is a personal process that does not necessarily lead to the same relationship dynamics as before.

4. **External Judgments and Pressure:** Others may not be ready or willing to forgive, which can lead to external judgments, strained relationships, or pressure to conform to societal expectations of forgiveness.

5. **Emotional Vulnerability:** Engaging in the forgiveness process requires vulnerability and openness, which can be challenging for some individuals and may bring up difficult emotions during the healing journey.

Chapter 2: The Significance of Knowing Your Goal.

Having a clear sense of purpose and direction in life is crucial for personal growth, fulfillment, and success. The ability to identify and pursue meaningful goals provides individuals with motivation, focus, and a sense of accomplishment. In this essay, we will explore the importance of knowing your goal and how it impacts various aspects of life.

1. Clarity and Focus.

Knowing your goal brings clarity and focus to your life. When you have a clear objective in mind, you can direct your energy and efforts towards achieving it. This clarity eliminates distractions and helps you make better decisions aligned with your purpose. Without a goal, you may find yourself drifting aimlessly, lacking motivation, and feeling unfulfilled. With a goal in sight, you gain a sense of direction, and every action you take becomes purposeful.

2. Motivation and Determination.

A well-defined goal serves as a powerful motivator. It provides a sense of purpose, ignites passion, and fuels determination. When you know what you want to achieve, you are more likely to stay committed and persevere through challenges and setbacks. Goals act as a driving force, pushing you to go beyond your limits, overcome obstacles, and reach new heights. They give you a reason to wake up each day with enthusiasm and work towards creating a better future.

3. Measuring Progress and Success.

Having a clear goal allows you to measure your progress and determine your level of success. When you set specific, measurable goals, you can track your achievements and milestones along the way. This tracking process provides a sense of accomplishment and satisfaction as you witness your progress. Additionally, it enables you to make adjustments and improvements, ensuring you stay on the right path towards achieving your ultimate objective.

4. Personal Growth and Development.

Knowing your goal opens doors for personal growth and development. Pursuing a goal requires you to step out of your comfort zone, acquire new skills, and face challenges that push you to develop as an individual. The journey towards your goal exposes you to new experiences, broadens your perspective, and enhances your knowledge and abilities. It encourages self-reflection, self-improvement, and personal transformation. The process of striving towards a goal allows you to discover your strengths, overcome weaknesses, and unlock your full potential.

5. Alignment with Values and Passions.

When you have a clear goal, you can align it with your values and passions. Understanding what truly matters to you enables you to set meaningful objectives that resonate with your core beliefs and desires. When your goals align with your values, you experience a deeper sense of fulfillment and satisfaction. Moreover, pursuing goals that are connected to your passions brings joy and enthusiasm to your endeavors, making the journey more enjoyable and rewarding.

Tips for the Significance of Knowing Your Goal.

1. **Self-reflection:** Take time to reflect on your values, passions, and aspirations. Understand what truly matters to you and what you want to achieve in different areas of your life.
2. **Set SMART goals:** Ensure your goals are Specific, Measurable, Attainable, Relevant, and Time-bound. This framework helps you create clear and actionable objectives.
3. **Prioritize:** Determine which goals are most important to you and prioritize them accordingly. Focus your energy and resources on the goals that align with your values and have the greatest impact on your life.
4. **Break it down:** Break your long-term goals into smaller, manageable tasks. This approach makes them less overwhelming and allows you to track your progress more effectively.

5. **Write it down:** Document your goals in writing. This practice solidifies your commitment and serves as a constant reminder of what you're striving for.

6. **Create an action plan:** Develop a step-by-step plan to achieve each goal. Identify the resources, skills, and support needed to accomplish them.

7. **Review and adjust:** Regularly review your goals and make adjustments as necessary. Life circumstances change, and your goals may need to be modified to stay aligned with your evolving aspirations.

8. **Stay accountable:** Share your goals with a trusted friend, mentor, or accountability partner. Their support and encouragement can help you stay motivated and committed.

9. **Celebrate milestones:** Acknowledge and celebrate your achievements along the way. This practice boosts morale and reinforces your progress, providing additional motivation to continue working towards your goals.

10. **Stay resilient:** Embrace setbacks and failures as opportunities for growth. Learn from them, adapt your approach, and persevere despite obstacles.

Benefits of the Significance of Knowing Your Goal.

1. **Clarity and focus:** Knowing your goal provides clarity and focus, allowing you to make informed decisions and take purposeful actions.

2. **Motivation and drive:** Having a clear goal fuels motivation and determination, propelling you to overcome challenges and stay committed.

3. **Sense of fulfillment:** Achieving your goals brings a sense of fulfillment and satisfaction, boosting your overall well-being.

4. **Personal growth and development:** Pursuing goals pushes you to expand your skills, knowledge, and abilities, fostering personal growth and development.

5. **Improved decision-making:** Knowing your goal helps you make decisions aligned with your long-term objectives, avoiding distractions and short-term gratification.

6. **Enhanced productivity:** Having a goal increases your productivity as you focus your efforts on tasks that contribute to its achievement.

7. **Increased self-confidence:** Progressing towards and achieving your goals boosts self-confidence and self-belief.

8. **Better time management:** Knowing your goal allows you to prioritize tasks and manage your time effectively, ensuring efficient progress.

9. **Stronger sense of purpose:** Goals provide a sense of purpose, giving your life direction and meaning.

10. **Resilience and adaptability:** Having a goal fosters resilience and adaptability in the face of challenges, as you remain committed to your long-term vision.

Functions of the Significance of Knowing Your Goal.

1. **Direction:** Goals provide a sense of direction, guiding your actions and decisions.
2. **Measurement:** Goals allow you to measure your progress and determine your level of success.
3. **Focus:** Goals help you concentrate your efforts on specific areas, minimizing distractions.
4. **Motivation:** Goals act as powerful motivators, driving you to take action and overcome obstacles.
5. **Planning:** Goals facilitate the creation of action plans, outlining the steps needed to achieve them.
6. **Evaluation:** Goals provide a framework for self-assessment, allowing you to evaluate your performance and make improvements.
7. **Inspiration:** Goals inspire you to reach for higher levels of achievement and strive for excellence.
8. **Collaboration:** Goals can foster collaboration and teamwork, as individuals work together towards a common objective.
9. **Adaptability:** Goals require adaptability, as you may need to adjust your approach based on changing circumstances.
10. **Satisfaction:** Goals contribute to a sense of satisfaction and fulfillment when achieved, providing a sense of accomplishment.

Techniques of the Significance of Knowing Your Goal.

1. **Visualization:** Use visualization techniques to create a mental image of your desired outcome. This helps solidify your goal and increases motivation to work towards it.

2. **Goal Setting: Employ effective** goal-setting techniques, such as SMART goals (Specific, Measurable, Attainable, Relevant, Time-bound), to ensure clarity and actionable objectives.

3. **Action Planning:** Develop a detailed action plan that outlines the specific steps needed to achieve your goal. Breaking it down into manageable tasks makes it more attainable.

4. **Time Management:** Implement time management techniques to prioritize tasks, allocate time effectively, and ensure progress towards your goal.

5. **Self-Discipline:** Cultivate self-discipline to stay focused and committed to your goal, even when faced with distractions or challenges.

6. **Continuous Learning:** Embrace a growth mindset and commit to continuous learning. Acquiring new knowledge and skills can propel you towards your goal.

7. **Accountability:** Establish accountability mechanisms, such as sharing your goals with a trusted friend or mentor, to hold yourself responsible for your progress.

8. **Networking:** Build a supportive network of individuals who share similar goals or can provide guidance and support along your journey.

9. **Positive Affirmations:** Practice positive affirmations to reinforce your belief in your ability to achieve your goal. Affirmations can help overcome self-doubt and increase confidence.

10. **Reflection and Evaluation:** Regularly reflect on your progress, evaluate your actions, and make adjustments if necessary. This self-reflection aids in staying on track towards your goal.

Factors of the Significance of Knowing Your Goal.

1. **Clarity:** Having a clear understanding of your goal is essential. Clearly defining what you want to achieve helps eliminate ambiguity and confusion.

2. **Passion:** A goal that aligns with your passions and interests provides intrinsic motivation, making it easier to stay committed and overcome obstacles.

3. **Self-Awareness:** Being self-aware allows you to identify your strengths, weaknesses, and areas for improvement. This knowledge can inform your goal-setting process.

4. **Values Alignment:** Ensure that your goal aligns with your core values. When your goals are in harmony with your values, you experience a greater sense of fulfillment.

5. **External Motivation:** External factors, such as support from loved ones or recognition from peers, can serve as additional motivation to achieve your goal.

6. **Resilience:** Resilience is crucial in the face of challenges and setbacks. Cultivating resilience helps you bounce back and continue pursuing your goal.

7. **Resources:** Access to resources, such as finances, time, knowledge, and supportive networks, can significantly influence goal attainment.

8. **Environment:** The environment you surround yourself with can impact your goal pursuit. A positive and supportive environment can foster success.

9. **Commitment:** Wholehearted commitment and dedication to your goal are vital factors in achieving it. Without commitment, progress may be hindered.

10. **Flexibility:** Being open to adapting your approach or adjusting your goal, while staying true to its essence, can increase the likelihood of success.

Causes of the Significance of Knowing Your Goal.

1. **Personal Aspirations:** Goals are often driven by personal aspirations, desires, and dreams for the future.

2. **External Influences:** External factors, such as societal expectations, cultural norms, or career opportunities, can influence the goals individuals set.

3. **Life Experiences:** Past experiences, both positive and negative, can shape an individual's goals. Lessons learned from previous endeavors can inform future aspirations.

4. **Personal Values:** Individuals often set goals that align with their personal values, principles, and beliefs.

5. **Desire for Growth:** The innate desire for personal growth and self-improvement can be a cause for setting meaningful goals.

6. **Overcoming Challenges:** Goals may be set as a means to overcome specific challenges or obstacles that individuals face in their lives.

7. **Passion and Interests:** Goals are often born out of individuals' passions, interests, and hobbies. Pursuing what brings joy and fulfillment can be a driving force.

8. **External Recognition:** The desire for external recognition or validation can lead individuals to set goals that showcase their abilities or achievements.

9. **Economic Factors:** Economic considerations, such as financial stability or career advancement, can be a cause for setting specific goals.

10. **Personal Fulfillment:** Goals are often set to achieve a sense of personal fulfillment, happiness, and satisfaction in life.

Importance of the Significance of Knowing Your Goal.

1. **Direction:** It provides you with a clear sense of direction and purpose. It helps you make decisions and prioritize tasks that align with your desired outcome.

2. **Motivation:** Having a clearly defined goal keeps you motivated and focused on achieving it. It gives meaning to your efforts and helps overcome obstacles.

3. **Progress measurement:** Knowing your goal allows you to measure your progress and gauge how far you've come. It

helps you stay on track and make necessary adjustments along the way.

Qualities of the Significance of Knowing Your Goal.

1. **Clarity:** A well-defined goal is specific, measurable, achievable, relevant, and time-bound (SMART). It helps you have a clear understanding of what you want to achieve.
2. **Personal alignment:** Your goal should align with your values, passions, and long-term aspirations. It should resonate with you and bring a sense of fulfillment.
3. **Realistic:** While it's beneficial to set ambitious goals, they should also be realistic and attainable. This ensures you stay motivated and don't get discouraged by setting unattainable targets.

Framework of the Significance of Knowing Your Goal.

1. **Identify your passions and interests:** Start by understanding what truly matters to you and what you are passionate about. This will help you align your goals with your personal values.
2. **Set specific goals:** Define your goals in a specific and measurable manner. Break them down into smaller milestones for easier tracking and accomplishment.
3. **Plan of action:** Create a roadmap or plan of action to achieve your goals. Break it down into actionable steps, set deadlines, and allocate resources effectively.

4. **Monitor and adapt:** Regularly review your progress and adjust your plans if needed. Stay flexible and open to changes to ensure continuous growth and improvement.

Pros of the Significance of Knowing Your Goal.

1. **Direction:** Knowing your goal provides you with a clear sense of direction and purpose.
2. **Motivation:** It keeps you motivated and focused on achieving your desired outcome.
3. **Progress tracking:** It allows you to measure your progress and make necessary adjustments.
4. **Decision-making:** Knowing your goal helps you make decisions that align with your desired outcome.
5. **Prioritization:** It helps you prioritize tasks and allocate time and resources effectively.
6. **Clarity:** Having a well-defined goal brings clarity to your actions and decisions.
7. **Personal growth:** It provides an opportunity for personal development and growth.
8. **Efficiency:** Having a goal helps you avoid distractions and stay focused on what matters.
9. **Confidence:** Knowing your goal boosts your confidence as you work toward its accomplishment.
10. **Sense of fulfillment:** Achieving your goal brings a sense of fulfillment and satisfaction.

Cons of the Significance of Knowing Your Goal.

1. **Rigidity:** Being too focused on a given goal can make you less adaptable to changing circumstances.

2. **Tunnel vision:** Overemphasis on a single goal might cause you to overlook other valuable opportunities.

3. **Potential disappointment:** Failing to achieve a goal can lead to disappointment or demotivation.

4. **Unrealistic expectations:** Setting overly ambitious goals may result in frustration if they are not attainable.

5. **Pressure and stress:** Pursuing goals can potentially increase pressure and stress levels.

6. **Lack of flexibility:** Goals may limit your ability to explore alternative paths or possibilities.

7. **Time constraints:** Goals can create time constraints and potentially restrict your ability to take breaks or explore new interests.

8. **Overlooking other aspects of life:** Focusing solely on goals may cause you to neglect other important aspects of life, such as relationships or personal well-being.

9. **Comparison and competition:** Goal-oriented individuals might experience increased competition and comparison with others, leading to additional stress.

10. **Potential burnout:** Being intensely goal-focused can increase the risk of burnout if you do not take breaks or practice self-care.

Chapter 3: Close In on Your Objective.

The Key to Success.

In our journey towards achieving our goals, we often encounter challenges and obstacles that may divert us from our intended path. However, by adopting a focused and determined mindset, we can close in on our objectives and pave the way to success. This essay aims to provide insights into the significance of focusing on our objectives and exploring strategies that can help us remain committed to our goals.

1. Understanding Objectives.

To close in on our objectives, it is crucial to have a clear understanding of what we want to achieve. Objectives serve as guiding beacons, providing direction and purpose to our endeavours. When setting objectives, it is important to make them specific, measurable, attainable, relevant, and time-bound, also known as SMART goals. By setting SMART goals, we gain clarity on our intentions and create a framework for monitoring our progress.

2. The Power of Focus.

Focus plays a pivotal role in our ability to close in on our objectives. It enables us to channel our energy and resources towards what truly matters, eliminating unnecessary distractions. When we focus on our goals, we become more efficient, productive, and resilient in the face of challenges. By investing our time and efforts in activities that align with our desired outcomes, we maximize our chances of success. Moreover, focus enhances our decision-making abilities, as it helps us prioritize and make informed choices that propel us closer to our objectives.

3. Developing a Growth Mindset.

Closing in on our objectives requires a growth mindset, embracing challenges, learning from failures, and persisting in the pursuit of our goals. With a growth mindset, we view setbacks as opportunities for growth, rather than insurmountable barriers. We develop resilience, adaptability, and a willingness to continuously learn and improve. Cultivating a growth mindset allows us to approach our objectives with optimism and perseverance, even in the face of adversity.

4. Strategies to Close In on Objectives.

To ensure we stay on track and close in on our objectives, we can adopt several strategies:

- **Break it Down:** Breaking down our objectives into smaller, actionable steps makes them more manageable and less overwhelming. By focusing on one step at a time, we maintain clarity and constantly progress towards our ultimate goal.

- **Time Management:** Effective time management is essential in closing in on objectives. Prioritization, setting deadlines, and allocating dedicated time slots for specific tasks create structure and help us make steady progress. Moreover, taking regular breaks and maintaining a work-life balance keeps us motivated and prevents burnout.

- **Accountability and Support:** Sharing our objectives with trusted individuals who can hold us accountable can significantly increase our commitment and drive. Whether it's a mentor, coach, or a support group, seeking external support and feedback helps us stay focused and motivated throughout our journey.

- **Continuous Evaluation and Adaptation:** It is crucial to assess our progress regularly and make adjustments when necessary. Reflecting on our actions, identifying what works and what doesn't, and making necessary adaptations ensures we stay on the right track towards our objectives.

Tips that can enhance your chances of success.

1. **Set Clear Goals:** Clearly define what you want to achieve to stay focused and motivated.

2. **Plan Strategically:** Develop a well-structured plan that outlines the steps required to reach your goals.

3. **Take Action:** Take consistent and purposeful action towards your objectives to make progress.

4. **Learn from Mistakes:** Embrace failure as an opportunity to learn and improve your future strategies.

5. **Stay Persistent:** Persist through challenges and setbacks, maintaining determination to reach your objective.

6. **Embrace Discipline:** Cultivate self-discipline to stay on track and avoid distractions.

7. **Seek Feedback:** Regularly seek feedback from mentors, peers, or experts to refine your approach.

8. **Adapt and Flexibility:** Be willing to adapt your plans and strategies based on changing circumstances.

9. **Continuous Learning:** Invest in gathering knowledge and skills to enhance your performance.

10. **Stay Positive:** Maintain a positive mindset, as optimism can help overcome obstacles and fuel your motivation.

Benefits that can be derived from focusing on your objective.

1. **Increased Motivation:** When you focus on your objective, your motivation levels naturally rise.

2. **Enhanced Clarity:** Setting a specific objective provides a clear sense of direction and purpose.

3. **Improved Time Management:** By focusing on your objective, you prioritize tasks more effectively.

4. **Boosted Confidence:** Making progress towards your objective boosts self-assurance and belief in your abilities.

5. **Greater Resilience:** Focusing on your objective strengthens your ability to bounce back from failures or setbacks.

6. **Better Decision-Making:** When you have a clear objective, decision-making becomes more straightforward.

7. **Increased Productivity:** Concentrating on your objective helps minimize distractions and increases productivity.

8. **Improved Focus:** Having a specific objective sharpens your focus on what truly matters.

9. **Enhanced Self-Discipline:** Focusing on your objective requires discipline, which can be developed and refined.

10. **Personal Growth:** Working towards your objective helps you develop skills, knowledge, and experience.

Functions that closely align with focusing on your objective.

1. **Directional Guidance:** Your objective provides a clear direction and guidance for your actions.

2. **Prioritization:** Focusing on your objective helps you prioritize tasks and allocate resources efficiently.

3. **Decision Framework:** Having a specific objective creates a framework for making decisions.

4. **Accountability:** Working towards your objective creates a sense of personal accountability.

5. **Measurement:** Your objective serves as a benchmark for measuring progress and success.

6. **Feedback Loop:** Monitoring your progress towards your objective allows for adjustments and improvement.

7. **Adaptation:** Focusing on your objective helps you adapt to changing circumstances and make necessary changes.

8. **Alignment:** A clear objective aligns your actions and efforts towards a common goal.

9. **Motivation:** Your objective serves as a source of motivation and drive to keep pushing forward.

10. **Performance Evaluation:** Focusing on your objective allows for self-assessment and evaluation of your performance.

Techniques to Get Closer to Your Objectives.

1. **Goal Setting:** Clearly define your objectives and break them down into manageable tasks.

2. **Planning:** Develop a well-structured plan that outlines how you will achieve your objectives.

3. **Prioritization:** Identify the most important tasks and allocate your time and resources accordingly.

4. **Focus:** Concentrate your energy and attention on one task at a time to increase productivity.

5. **Time Management:** Efficiently allocate your time by setting deadlines and avoiding distractions.

6. **Action Orientation:** Take consistent action towards your objectives to make progress.

7. **Adaptability:** Be flexible and open to adjusting your approach based on feedback and circumstances.

8. **Continuous Learning:** Seek knowledge and actively develop new skills relevant to your objectives.

9. **Networking:** Build relationships with like-minded individuals who can offer support and resources.

10. **Perseverance:** Stay committed and resilient in the face of obstacles or setbacks.

Factors that Contribute to Success.

1. **Clarity of Purpose:** Having a clear understanding of what you want to achieve.

2. **Self-Motivation:** Cultivating the drive and determination to pursue your objectives.

3. **Discipline:** Consistently following through with your plans and staying focused.

4. **Resilience:** Bouncing back from failures and setbacks without losing enthusiasm.

5. **Positive Mindset:** Maintaining an optimistic outlook and believing in your abilities.

6. **Accountability:** Taking responsibility for your actions and outcomes.

7. **Effective Communication:** Clearly conveying your thoughts, ideas, and needs to others.

8. **Emotional Intelligence:** Understanding and managing your emotions, as well as empathizing with others.

9. **Adaptability:** Being able to adjust and thrive in changing circumstances.

10. **Continuous Improvement:** Constantly seeking ways to enhance your skills and performance.

Causes that Drive Success.

1. **Passion:** Having a strong sense of enthusiasm and enjoyment for what you are pursuing.
2. **Hard Work:** Putting in the necessary effort and going the extra mile to achieve your goals.
3. **Perseverance:** Persisting through challenges and maintaining your determination.
4. **Self-Belief:** Having confidence in your abilities and trusting yourself.
5. **Planning and Organization:** Structuring your activities and resources effectively.
6. **Focus on Excellence:** Striving for high-quality outcomes and continuous improvement.
7. **Learning from Failure:** Embracing setbacks as opportunities for growth and learning.
8. **Supportive Environment:** Surrounding yourself with people who encourage and inspire you.
9. **Taking Calculated Risks:** Identifying and seizing opportunities that can propel you forward.
10. **Adaptability to Change:** Embracing change and being open to new strategies and ideas.

Pros of the Key to Success.

1. **Provides clarity and focus:** Having a clear objective helps you stay focused on what you want to achieve, increasing your chances of success.

2. **Motivates and drives you:** Knowing your objective gives you a sense of purpose and motivation to overcome obstacles and work towards achieving it.

3. **Enhances decision-making:** With a defined objective, you can make better decisions that align with your end goal and bring you closer to success.

4. **Increases productivity:** Having a clear objective allows you to set targets and deadlines, boosting productivity as you work towards achieving them.

5. **Measures progress and success:** Objectives act as benchmarks against which you can measure your progress and determine whether you are on track to achieving your goals.

6. **Aids in resource allocation:** When you know your objective, you can allocate resources – such as time, money, and manpower – more efficiently to achieve optimal results.

7. **Promotes accountability:** Clearly stated objectives hold you accountable for your actions and provide a foundation for others to hold you accountable as well.

8. **Boosts personal and professional growth:** By working towards your objective, you learn new skills, gain experience, and develop personally and professionally.

9. **Drives innovation:** Working towards a specific objective encourages creativity and out-of-the-box thinking, leading to innovative solutions and approaches.

10. **Provides a sense of fulfillment:** Achieving your objective brings a sense of accomplishment and fulfillment, boosting your confidence and satisfaction.

Cons of the Key to Success.

1. **Potential for tunnel vision:** Being too focused on your objective may cause you to overlook other opportunities or fail to adapt to changing circumstances.

2. **Lack of flexibility:** Having a rigid objective may limit your ability to adapt and adjust your plans as new information or challenges arise.

3. **Risk of burnout:** Being solely driven by your objective can lead to burnout if you neglect self-care and work excessively towards your goal.

4. **Potential for disappointment:** Failing to achieve your objective can lead to disappointment and feelings of failure if you are overly fixated on it.

5. **Neglecting other aspects of life:** Being too focused on your objective may cause you to neglect other important areas of your life, such as relationships or personal well-being.

Chapter 4: Strengthen Your Castle.

Building Resilience in an Ever-Changing World.

In life, we all have our own metaphorical castles — a sanctuary where we seek security, stability, and peace of mind. These castles symbolize our lives, relationships, careers, and overall well-being. However, the world is a dynamic place, constantly presenting challenges and uncertainties that can threaten the fortitude of our castles. To navigate this ever-changing landscape, we must actively endeavor to strengthen our castles, fortifying them against the winds of adversity. This essay explores the concept of strengthening one's castle and presents practical strategies to enhance resilience in the face of life's challenges.

1. Understanding the Castle of Self-awareness and Values.

- **Self-awareness:** Strengthening our castle begins with deep self-awareness. We must understand our strengths, weaknesses, fears, and aspirations. By gaining insight into ourselves, we can identify areas that require fortification and areas that can serve as foundations for resilience.

- **Values:** Our castle is anchored by our core values. These values guide our thoughts, actions, and decision-making processes. By clarifying our values, we can align ourselves with what truly matters, creating a solid foundation for personal growth and resilience.

2. Building Strong Foundations for Physical and Mental Well-being.

- **Physical well-being:** A strong castle requires a healthy body. Prioritizing physical fitness, nutrition, and sleep rejuvenates our energy levels, enhances productivity, and strengthens our ability to face challenges head-on.
- **Mental well-being:** A resilient castle also requires a strong mind. Cultivating mental well-being through practices like mindfulness, meditation, and self-reflection helps us manage stress, develop emotional intelligence, and maintain a positive outlook.

3. Fortifying Walls of Developing Coping Mechanisms.

- **Emotional resilience:** Emotional resilience equips us with the ability to bounce back from setbacks and adapt to change. Building emotional resilience involves cultivating self-compassion, fostering healthy relationships, and developing effective coping mechanisms to manage stress and adversity.

- **Cognitive resilience:** Cognitive resilience involves building mental toughness and a flexible mindset. By challenging negative thoughts, embracing a growth mindset, and seeking opportunities for learning and personal development, we strengthen our cognitive resilience and enhance our problem-solving abilities.

4. Investing in Relationships for the Strength of Social Support.

- **Building a support network:** Surrounding ourselves with a reliable support network is fundamental to maintaining a strong castle. Cultivating genuine connections, seeking emotional support, and nurturing meaningful relationships provide us with a safety net during challenging times.
- **Collaboration and teamwork:** Strengthening our castle also involves recognizing the power of collaboration and teamwork. By fostering positive relationships and engaging in collective problem-solving, we can pool resources and skills to overcome obstacles that might otherwise seem insurmountable.

5. Adapting to Change from Resilience in the Face of Adversity.

- **Embracing change:** Change is inevitable, and our ability to adapt to it is crucial. By cultivating a mindset of flexibility and embracing change as an opportunity for growth, we can navigate life's uncertainties with resilience and grace.

- **Learning from setbacks:** Setbacks and failures are integral parts of the journey to strengthen our castle. Viewing setbacks as opportunities for learning, practicing self-reflection, and adjusting our strategies empowers us to grow stronger and more resilient with each challenge we encounter.

Tips for Strengthening Your Castle and Building Resilience.

1. **Cultivate self-awareness:** Understand your strengths, weaknesses, values, and aspirations to lay a solid foundation for resilience.

2. **Prioritize physical well-being:** Take care of your body through regular exercise, healthy eating, and sufficient rest to enhance your energy levels and ability to withstand challenges.

3. **Nurture mental well-being:** Practice mindfulness, meditation, and self-reflection to manage stress, develop emotional intelligence, and maintain a positive mindset.

4. **Develop effective coping mechanisms:** Learn healthy ways to cope with stress, such as seeking support from loved ones, engaging in hobbies, or practicing relaxation techniques.

5. **Foster positive relationships:** Build a support network of reliable friends and family who can provide emotional support and guidance during difficult times.

6. **Embrace change:** Develop a flexible mindset that embraces change as an opportunity for growth and adaptation, rather than resisting or fearing it.

7. **Learn from setbacks:** View setbacks and failures as valuable learning experiences, allowing you to adjust strategies, grow stronger, and develop resilience.

8. **Practice self-compassion:** Be kind to yourself, acknowledging and accepting your imperfections while treating yourself with compassion and understanding.

9. **Seek growth and learning:** Embrace a growth mindset, continuously seeking opportunities for personal and professional development to enhance your problem-solving abilities.

10. **Maintain a positive outlook:** Cultivate optimism and gratitude, focusing on the positive aspects of your life and maintaining hope even in challenging situations.

Benefits of Strengthening Your Castle and Building Resilience.

1. **Increased psychological well-being:** Strengthening your castle enhances mental and emotional well-being, leading to greater happiness and life satisfaction.

2. **Improved stress management:** Resilience equips you with effective coping mechanisms to manage stress and bounce back from difficult situations.

3. **Enhanced problem-solving skills:** By developing resilience, you cultivate a flexible mindset and the ability to find creative solutions to challenges that arise.

4. **Better physical health:** Prioritizing physical well-being boosts your immune system, increases energy levels, and reduces the risk of chronic illnesses.

5. **Stronger relationships:** Building resilience allows you to navigate conflicts and setbacks in relationships more effectively, fostering healthier and more meaningful connections.
6. **Increased productivity:** Resilience helps you stay focused, motivated, and productive, even in the face of adversity.
7. **Greater adaptability:** Strengthening your castle enables you to adapt to change more readily, embracing new opportunities and navigating transitions with confidence.
8. **Improved decision-making:** Resilience enhances your ability to think rationally and make sound decisions, even when under pressure or in uncertain circumstances.
9. **Higher self-esteem:** Building resilience cultivates a sense of self-confidence and self-worth, enabling you to face challenges with belief in your abilities.
10. **Overall life satisfaction:** Strengthening your castle and developing resilience leads to a more fulfilling and satisfying life, as you feel equipped to face whatever comes your way.

Functions of a Strong Castle (Metaphorically).

1. **Shelter:** A strong castle provides a safe and secure space for personal growth, self-reflection, and rejuvenation.
2. **Protection:** It shields you from external stresses, setbacks, and negative influences, allowing you to maintain a sense of inner peace and stability.

3. **Resilience:** A fortified castle enables you to bounce back from adversity, setbacks, and challenges with increased strength and determination.

4. **Navigation:** It serves as a compass, guiding you through life's uncertainties and helping you make informed decisions.

5. **Support system:** A strong castle is built upon a foundation of supportive relationships, providing emotional support and guidance during difficult times.

6. **Adaptability:** Like a castle, resilience allows you to adapt to changing circumstances, embracing new opportunities and challenges with flexibility and confidence.

7. **Growth:** A fortified castle creates an environment conducive to personal growth, learning, and self-improvement.

8. **Emotional well-being:** A strong castle promotes emotional well-being, allowing you to manage stress, regulate emotions, and maintain a positive outlook.

9. **Connection:** It fosters connections with others, encouraging collaboration, teamwork, and the sharing of resources and skills.

10. **Fulfillment:** A fortified castle leads to a sense of fulfillment and satisfaction, as it enables you to live a life aligned with your values and aspirations.

Techniques for Strengthening Your Castle and Building Resilience.

1. **Mindfulness and Meditation:** Practice mindfulness and meditation to cultivate self-awareness, reduce stress, and enhance emotional well-being.

2. **Cognitive Restructuring:** Challenge negative thought patterns and replace them with more positive and realistic perspectives to build resilience and improve mental health.

3. **Physical Exercise:** Engage in regular physical exercise to boost mood, reduce stress, and increase overall resilience.

4. **Social Support:** Seek support from trusted friends, family members, or support groups to foster connection, receive guidance, and cope with challenges.

5. **Journaling:** Write down your thoughts, emotions, and experiences in a journal to gain clarity, process emotions, and promote self-reflection.

6. **Time Management:** Develop effective time management skills to prioritize tasks, reduce overwhelm, and enhance productivity, leading to increased resilience.

7. **Problem-Solving Skills:** Learn and practice problem-solving techniques to approach challenges systematically, identify solutions, and build resilience in handling obstacles.

8. **Self-care:** Prioritize self-care activities, such as relaxation, hobbies, and self-compassion, to recharge and nurture your physical and mental well-being.

9. **Positive Affirmations:** Use positive affirmations to reframe negative self-talk, boost self-confidence, and foster a resilient mindset.

10. **Seeking Professional Help:** When needed, don't hesitate to seek support from mental health professionals who can provide guidance, therapy, and tools for building resilience.

Factors Impacting the Strength of Your Castle and Resilience.

1. **Self-esteem and self-worth:** Individuals with higher self-esteem tend to be more resilient, as they have a stronger belief in their abilities to overcome challenges.

2. **Supportive Relationships:** Having a network of supportive relationships provides emotional support, encouragement, and a sense of belonging, contributing to resilience.

3. **Coping Mechanisms:** The effectiveness of coping mechanisms, such as problem-solving skills, emotional regulation, and seeking social support, influences resilience.

4. **Emotional Intelligence:** Emotional intelligence, including self-awareness, empathy, and emotional regulation, plays a significant role in building resilience.

5. **Previous Life Experiences:** Past experiences, including traumas, setbacks, and successes, can shape resilience by providing opportunities for growth and learning.

6. **Genetics and Biology:** Genetic factors can influence an individual's predisposition to resilience, while biological factors, such as stress response systems, impact resilience levels.

7. **Social and Cultural Factors:** Socioeconomic status, cultural values, and access to resources can influence resilience levels, as they affect the support and opportunities available.

8. **Personal Beliefs and Mindset:** Resilient individuals often possess a growth mindset, believing in their ability to learn, adapt, and overcome challenges.

9. **Education and Knowledge:** Acquiring knowledge, skills, and education empowers individuals to face challenges more effectively and build resilience.

10. **Environmental Factors:** Environmental factors, such as stability, safety, and access to basic needs, can impact an individual's capacity to build resilience.

Causes for the Weakening of Your Castle and Resilience.

1. **Chronic Stress:** Prolonged exposure to stress without effective coping mechanisms can weaken resilience over time.

2. **Traumatic Experiences:** Severe trauma can significantly impact resilience, making it more challenging to bounce back from adversity.

3. **Lack of Support:** Insufficient social support or a lack of nurturing relationships can weaken resilience and hinder the ability to navigate challenges.

4. **Negative Thinking Patterns:** Persistent negative thinking and self-criticism can erode resilience, fostering a defeatist mindset.

5. **Isolation and Loneliness:** Feeling isolated and lacking social connections can diminish resilience and make it harder to cope with difficulties.

6. **Unhealthy Coping Mechanisms:** Relying on unhealthy coping mechanisms, such as substance abuse or avoidance, can weaken resilience over time.

7. **Lack of Self-care:** Neglecting self-care activities can deplete energy levels, hinder emotional well-being, and contribute to decreased resilience.

8. **Limited Resources:** Lack of access to essential resources, such as education, healthcare, or social support, can hinder resilience-building efforts.

9. **Unresolved Past Traumas:** Unresolved past traumas can continue to impact resilience, making it harder to face new challenges.

10. **Negative Environments:** Being in toxic or unsupportive environments, such as an abusive relationship or a hostile work environment, can weaken resilience and erode well-being.

Importance of Strengthening Your Castle and Building Resilience.

1. **Emotional Well-being:** Building resilience enhances emotional well-being, allowing you to manage stress, regulate emotions, and maintain a positive outlook.

2. **Mental Health:** Resilience plays a crucial role in preventing and managing mental health issues, such as anxiety and depression.

3. **Adaptability:** Resilience enables you to adapt to change more readily, embracing new opportunities and navigating transitions with confidence.

4. **Coping with Challenges:** Strengthening your castle equips you with effective coping mechanisms to face and overcome challenges that arise in life.

5. **Personal Growth:** Building resilience fosters personal growth, as it encourages self-reflection, learning from setbacks, and embracing new experiences.

6. **Relationships:** Resilience strengthens your relationships by enabling you to navigate conflicts, setbacks, and changes with greater resilience and understanding.

7. **Professional Success:** Resilience is vital for professional success, as it enhances problem-solving skills, adaptability, and the ability to handle work-related stress.

8. **Physical Health:** Resilience positively impacts physical health by reducing stress-related illnesses, boosting immune function, and promoting healthy behaviors.

9. **Life Satisfaction:** Strengthening your castle and building resilience leads to a more fulfilling and satisfying life, as you feel equipped to face challenges and pursue your goals.

10. **Overall Well-being:** Resilience is a key component of overall well-being, contributing to a sense of balance, fulfillment, and fulfillment in life.

Qualities of a Strong Castle and Resilient Individual.

1. **Self-Awareness:** Resilient individuals possess a deep understanding of their strengths, weaknesses, values, and emotions, allowing them to navigate challenges effectively.

2. **Adaptability:** Resilient individuals are flexible and open-minded, able to adjust to new circumstances, and find creative solutions to problems.

3. **Optimism:** Resilient individuals maintain a positive outlook, seeing setbacks as temporary and opportunities for growth and learning.

4. **Emotional Intelligence:** Resilient individuals possess high emotional intelligence, allowing them to understand and regulate their emotions effectively.

5. **Problem-Solving Skills:** Resilient individuals are skilled problem solvers, able to approach challenges with a rational and strategic mindset.

6. **Self-Compassion:** Resilient individuals practice self-compassion, treating themselves with kindness and understanding during difficult times.

7. **Social Support:** Resilient individuals cultivate and maintain strong support networks, seeking help and guidance from trusted friends and family.

8. **Perseverance:** Resilient individuals demonstrate perseverance and determination, willing to put in the effort and bounce back from setbacks.

9. **Growth Mindset:** Resilient individuals possess a growth mindset, believing in their capacity to learn, grow, and improve through challenges.

10. **Self-Care:** Resilient individuals prioritize self-care activities to nurture their physical, mental, and emotional well-being.

Framework for Strengthening Your Castle and Building Resilience.

1. **Self-Reflection:** Engage in self-reflection to understand your strengths, weaknesses, and values, laying a foundation for resilience.

2. **Set Goals:** Define clear goals that align with your values and aspirations, providing a sense of purpose and direction.

3. **Develop Coping Strategies:** Identify and develop healthy coping strategies that work for you, such as seeking support, practicing mindfulness, or engaging in creative outlets.

4. **Build Supportive Relationships:** Cultivate supportive relationships with friends, family, mentors, or support groups to provide emotional support and guidance.

5. **Embrace Change:** Develop a mindset that embraces change as an opportunity for growth and adaptation, rather than resisting or fearing it.

6. **Learn from Setbacks:** View setbacks and failures as valuable learning experiences, allowing you to adjust strategies, grow stronger, and develop resilience.

7. **Practice Self-Compassion:** Be kind to yourself, acknowledging and accepting your imperfections while treating yourself with compassion and understanding.

8. **Seek Growth and Learning:** Embrace a growth mindset, continuously seeking opportunities for personal and professional development to enhance problem-solving abilities.

9. **Prioritize Well-being:** Take care of your physical, mental, and emotional well-being through exercise, healthy habits, and self-care activities.

10. **Maintain a Positive Outlook:** Cultivate optimism and gratitude, focusing on the positive aspects of your life and maintaining hope even in challenging situations.

Pros of Strengthening Your Castle and Building Resilience.

1. **Improved Mental Health:** Building resilience enhances mental well-being, reducing the risk of developing mental health issues like anxiety and depression.

2. **Effective Stress Management:** Resilience equips individuals with coping mechanisms to manage stress effectively, promoting a healthier and balanced lifestyle.

3. **Adaptability to Change:** Resilient individuals can navigate and adapt to changes more easily, embracing new opportunities and challenges with confidence.

4. **Better Problem-Solving Skills:** Strengthening resilience enhances problem-solving abilities, enabling individuals to find creative solutions to overcome obstacles.

5. **Enhanced Emotional Well-being:** Resilience fosters emotional intelligence, allowing individuals to understand and regulate their emotions, leading to greater emotional well-being.

6. **Stronger Relationships:** Building resilience improves communication skills, empathy, and conflict management abilities, fostering stronger and healthier relationships.

7. **Increased Productivity:** Resilient individuals are better equipped to handle work-related stress, leading to improved productivity and performance in professional settings.

8. **Personal Growth and Development:** Strengthening resilience promotes personal growth, self-reflection, and a willingness to learn from setbacks, leading to continuous improvement.

9. **Better Physical Health:** Resilience positively impacts physical health by reducing stress-related illnesses and promoting healthy lifestyle choices.

10. **Greater Life Satisfaction:** Building resilience contributes to a sense of fulfillment, satisfaction, and overall well-being in various aspects of life.

Cons of Strengthening Your Castle and Building Resilience.

1. **Requires Effort and Time:** Strengthening resilience is a continuous process that requires commitment, effort, and investment of time.

2. **Emotional Discomfort:** Building resilience may involve facing and processing difficult emotions or past traumas, which can be emotionally challenging.

3. **Uncertainty and Ambiguity:** Strengthening resilience means embracing uncertainty and ambiguity, which can be uncomfortable for some individuals.

4. **Need for Vulnerability:** Building resilience often requires individuals to be vulnerable, open to seeking support, and sharing their struggles with others.

5. **Potential for Disappointment:** Despite building resilience, there may still be instances where individuals experience setbacks or disappointments, which can be discouraging.

6. **Resistance from Others:** Not everyone may understand or support an individual's efforts to build resilience, leading to potential resistance or lack of encouragement.

7. **Initial Discomfort:** Building resilience may involve stepping out of one's comfort zone, which can initially be uncomfortable or anxiety-inducing.

8. **Need for Continuous Maintenance:** Resilience-building is an ongoing process that requires consistent practice and maintenance to sustain its benefits.

9. **Potential for Overwhelm:** In some cases, individuals may feel overwhelmed by the pressure to be resilient or to constantly bounce back from challenges.

10. **Possible Frustration:** It can be frustrating when the desired level of resilience is not achieved immediately, requiring patience and perseverance.

Advantages of Strengthening Your Castle and Building Resilience.

1. Improved Mental and Emotional Well-being.
2. Enhanced Coping Skills.
3. Adaptability to Change.
4. Stronger Relationships.
5. Increased Self-Confidence.
6. Better Problem-Solving Abilities.
7. Greater Professional Succe.
8. Improved Physical Healing.
9. Personal Growth and Development.
10. Higher Life Satisfaction.

Disadvantages of Strengthening Your Castle and Building Resilience.

1. Requires Effort and Time.
2. Emotional Discomfort.
3. Uncertainty and Ambiguity.
4. Need for Vulnerability.
5. Potential for Disappointment.
6. Resistance from Others.
7. Initial Discomfort.
8. Need for Continuous Maintenance.
9. Potential for Overwhelm.
10. Possible Frustration.

Chapter 5: Control Your Thoughts.

Harnessing the Power of Cognitive Self-Regulation.

The human mind is a powerful tool that shapes our perceptions, emotions, and actions. Our thoughts have the ability to influence our experiences and ultimately determine our quality of life. However, without conscious effort, our thoughts can often become unruly, leading to negative thinking patterns, self-sabotage, and emotional distress. Hence, it is crucial to recognize the importance of controlling our thoughts and cultivating cognitive self-regulation. This essay will explore the significance of thought control, discuss the benefits it brings, provide practical strategies to achieve it, and examine its impact on various aspects of life.

1. Understanding Thought Control.

- Definition of thought control.
- The relationship between thoughts, emotions, and behaviors.
- The impact of uncontrolled thoughts on mental well-being.

2. The Benefits of Controlling Your Thoughts.

- Improved Emotional Well-being.
- Reduction in anxiety and stress levels.
- Enhanced ability to manage negative emotions.
- Increased resilience in the face of challenges.
- Enhanced Mental Health.
- Prevention of negative thinking patterns.
- Reduction in rumination and overthinking.
- Promotion of positive self-esteem and self-confidence.
- Improved Decision Making.
- Enhanced clarity and focus.
- Reduced impulsivity and better judgment.
- Increased ability to consider multiple perspectives.

3. Strategies for Thought Control.

- Mindfulness and Awareness.
- Cultivating present-moment awareness.
- Recognizing and acknowledging negative thoughts.
- Practicing non-judgmental observation of thought.
- Cognitive Restructuring.
- Identifying and challenging negative thought patterns
- Replacing negative thoughts with positive or realistic alternatives.
- Utilizing affirmations and positive self-talk.
- Emotional Regulation.
- Developing emotional intelligence.
- Identifying and managing triggers for negative emotions.

- Utilizing relaxation techniques and stress management strategies.
- Surrounding Yourself with Positivity.
- Engaging in positive social interactions.
- Consuming uplifting and inspiring content.
- Creating an environment that supports positive thinking.

6. The Impact of Thought Control on Different Aspects of Life.

- Relationships.
- Improved communication and conflict resolution.
- Increased empathy and understanding.
- Enhanced ability to maintain healthy boundaries.
- Personal Growth and Achievement.
- Increased motivation and goal-directed behavior.
- Overcoming self-doubt and fear of failure.
- Embracing continuous learning and development.
- Physical Health.
- Reduction in stress-related physical symptoms.
- Enhanced immune system functioning.
- Promotion of healthy habits and self-care practices.
- Professional Success.
- Improved focus and productivity.
- Increased ability to handle workplace stress.
- Enhanced problem-solving and decision-making skills.

Tips for Controlling Your Thoughts.

1. **Practice Mindfulness:** Cultivate present-moment awareness to observe your thoughts without judgment and detach from negative or unhelpful thinking patterns.

2. **Challenge Negative Thoughts:** Identify and question negative thoughts, examining their validity and replacing them with more rational and positive alternatives.

3. **Use Positive Affirmations:** Utilize positive self-talk and affirmations to counteract negative thoughts and reinforce empowering beliefs about yourself and your abilities.

4. **Engage in Cognitive Restructuring:** Reframe negative thoughts and reinterpret situations in a more positive and realistic light, fostering a healthier perspective.

5. **Develop Emotional Intelligence:** Enhance your ability to recognize and regulate your emotions, preventing them from influencing and controlling your thoughts.

6. **Practice Gratitude:** Focus on the positive aspects of your life and cultivate gratitude, shifting your mindset towards appreciation and contentment.

7. **Surround Yourself with Positivity:** Surround yourself with supportive and uplifting individuals, consume positive media content, and create an environment that fosters positive thinking.

8. **Set Realistic Expectations:** Avoid perfectionism and set realistic expectations for yourself, allowing for flexibility and self-compassion when faced with challenges or setbacks.

9. **Limit Exposure to Negative Influences:** Minimize exposure to negative news, toxic relationships, and environments that fuel negative thinking patterns.

10. **Seek Professional Help:** If you find it challenging to control your thoughts or if they significantly impact your well-being, consider seeking guidance from a mental health professional.

Benefits of Controlling Your Thoughts.

1. **Reduced Anxiety and Stress Levels:** By controlling negative and intrusive thoughts, you can reduce anxiety and stress, promoting a sense of calm and well-being.

2. **Improved Emotional Well-being:** Thought control allows you to manage your emotions more effectively, leading to increased happiness, contentment, and emotional stability.

3. **Enhanced Focus and Concentration:** When you control your thoughts, you can maintain better focus and concentration, improving productivity and performance in various tasks.

4. **Greater Self-Confidence:** By challenging negative thoughts and cultivating positive self-talk, you can boost self-confidence and belief in your abilities.

5. **Improved Decision-Making:** Thought control enhances clarity of thought and reduces impulsive decision-making, leading to more thoughtful and rational choices.

6. **Enhanced Problem-Solving Skills:** By controlling negative thoughts and reframing challenges, you can approach

problems with a clearer mindset and develop effective solutions.

7. **Increased Resilience:** Thought control fosters resilience by helping you bounce back from setbacks, adapt to change, and maintain a positive outlook.

8. **Better Relationships:** By controlling negative thoughts and emotions, you can communicate more effectively, manage conflicts, and build healthier and more fulfilling relationships.

9. **Greater Overall Well-being:** Thought control contributes to overall well-being by promoting a positive mindset, reducing stress-related health issues, and cultivating a sense of fulfillment.

10. **Personal Growth and Success:** By controlling your thoughts, you can overcome self-limiting beliefs, embrace challenges, and unlock your potential for personal growth and success.

Functions of Thought Control.

1. **Filtering:** Thought control allows you to filter out negative or unhelpful thoughts, focusing on those that are positive, constructive, and aligned with your goals.

2. **Reinterpretation:** Thought control enables you to reinterpret situations in a more positive and empowering light, altering the meaning you assign to them.

3. **Rational Thinking:** By controlling your thoughts, you can engage in rational thinking, making decisions based on logic and evidence rather than emotional biases.

4. **Emotional Regulation:** Thought control helps regulate your emotions by preventing negative thoughts from triggering intense emotional responses.

5. **Self-Reflection:** Through thought control, you can engage in self-reflection, examining your thoughts and beliefs to gain insights into your behaviors and motivations.

6. **Intention Setting:** By controlling your thoughts, you can set positive intentions for your actions, guiding your behaviors towards desired outcomes.

7. **Cognitive Restructuring:** Thought control facilitates cognitive restructuring, enabling you to reframe negative thoughts and replace them with more positive and rational ones.

8. **Problem-Solving:** By directing your thoughts, you can engage in effective problem-solving, finding creative solutions to challenges and obstacles.

9. **Focus and Concentration:** Thought control enhances your ability to focus and concentrate, allowing you to direct your attention where it is most needed.

10. **Self-Empowerment:** By controlling your thoughts, you take control of your own narrative and empower yourself to shape your experiences and outcomes.

Techniques you can use to harness the power of cognitive self-regulation.

1. **Mindfulness:** Practice staying present and aware of your thoughts and emotions.
2. **Meditation:** Set aside time for quiet reflection and mental relaxation.
3. **Cognitive restructuring:** Challenge and reframe negative or unhelpful thoughts.
4. **Goal setting:** Define clear objectives to guide your thoughts and actions.
5. **Time management:** Prioritize tasks and allocate time for focused work.
6. **Mental rehearsal:** Visualize successful outcomes and actions before executing them.
7. **Self-reflection:** Regularly assess your thoughts, behaviors, and progress.
8. **Self-talk:** Use positive and empowering language when speaking to yourself.
9. **Emotional regulation:** Develop strategies to manage and express emotions effectively.
10. **Physical well-being:** Maintain a healthy diet, exercise regularly, and get enough rest.

Factors that can influence cognitive self-regulation.

1. **Motivation:** Having a strong drive and desire to regulate your thoughts effectively.

2. **Self-awareness:** Understanding your strengths, weaknesses, and thought patterns.

3. **Environment:** Creating a conducive space for focused and distraction-free thinking.

4. **Social support:** Surrounding yourself with people who encourage and motivate you.

5. **Emotional intelligence:** Recognizing and managing your own emotions and others'.

6. **Beliefs and values:** Aligning your thoughts and actions with your principles.

7. **Resilience:** Bouncing back from setbacks and maintaining a positive mindset.

8. **Self-discipline:** Exercising self-control and resisting distractions or temptations.

9. **Learning and growth mindset:** Viewing challenges as opportunities for growth.

10. **Sleep and rest:** Ensuring adequate rest to replenish cognitive resources.

Importance of harnessing the power of cognitive self-regulation.

1. **Improved focus and attention:** Cognitive self-regulation helps you direct and maintain your focus on relevant tasks or thoughts while filtering out distractions.

2. **Enhanced decision-making:** By regulating your thoughts, you can think more clearly, consider different perspectives, and make more informed decisions.

3. **Increased emotional well-being:** Self-regulation allows you to manage and regulate your emotions effectively, leading to greater emotional resilience and well-being.

4. **Enhanced productivity:** By regulating your thoughts, you can prioritize tasks, manage time efficiently, and maintain a consistent level of productivity.

5. **Improved overall mental health:** Cognitive self-regulation can reduce anxiety, stress, and negative thought patterns, contributing to overall mental well-being.

Qualities that can support cognitive self-regulation.

1. **Self-awareness:** Being aware of your own thoughts, emotions, and triggers is crucial for effective self-regulation.

2. **Self-discipline:** Having the ability to control impulses and stay committed to your goals and strategies for self-regulation.

3. **Adaptability:** Being open to change and adjusting your thoughts or strategies as needed to meet your self-regulation goals.

4. **Resilience:** Developing the capacity to bounce back from setbacks or distractions and stay on track with your self-regulation efforts.

5. **Positive mindset:** Cultivating a positive attitude and optimism can help maintain motivation and persistence in regulating your thoughts.

Framework for cognitive self-regulation.

1. **Set clear goals:** Identify what specific thoughts or behaviors you want to regulate and define measurable objectives.

2. **Monitor your thoughts:** Regularly observe and evaluate your thoughts and mental processes to identify patterns, triggers, and areas for improvement.

3. **Identify strategies:** Explore and experiment with different techniques and approaches for cognitive self-regulation that align with your goals and preferences.

4. **Implement strategies:** Consistently apply the chosen strategies and techniques to regulate your thoughts and redirect them towards your desired outcomes.

5. **Evaluate and adjust:** Continuously assess the effectiveness of your strategies and make adjustments as needed to optimize your cognitive self-regulation process.

Pros / Advantages.

1. Improved focus and concentration, leading to better performance in tasks.

2. Enhanced decision-making skills and critical thinking abilities.

3. Increased emotional control and resilience in the face of challenges.

4. Improved self-awareness and understanding of one's thoughts and behaviors.

5. Greater ability to manage stress and reduce anxiety levels.

6. Improved productivity and time management skills.

7. Enhanced creativity and problem-solving abilities.

8. Increased mental well-being and overall happiness.

9. Greater sense of self-control and empowerment.

10. Improved relationships with others due to effective communication and emotional regulation.

Cons / Disadvantages.

1. Requires consistent effort and practice to develop effective self-regulation skills.

2. Can be challenging to maintain self-discipline and resist temptations or distractions.

3. Initial difficulty in identifying and understanding one's own cognitive patterns.

4. Requires effort to replace negative thought patterns with positive ones.

5. May take time to see tangible results and improvements.

6. Possible resistance or skepticism from others who do not understand the concept.

7. Requires active monitoring and constant evaluation of one's thoughts and behaviors.

8. Risk of becoming overly self-critical or putting excessive pressure on oneself.

9. Possible difficulty in adapting to new strategies or adjusting existing ones.

10. May initially feel uncomfortable or unfamiliar due to the need for change and self-reflection.

Chapter 6: Recognize Your Destructive Patterns and End Them.

Recognizing and ending destructive patterns is a crucial step towards personal growth and self-improvement. These patterns can manifest in various aspects of our lives, including relationships, habits, and thought patterns. By becoming aware of these destructive patterns, we can take steps to break free from their grip and create a more fulfilling and positive life. This essay will explore the concept of destructive patterns, their various forms, the impact they can have on our lives, and strategies to recognize and ultimately end them.

1. Understanding Destructive Patterns.

Destructive patterns refer to repetitive behaviors, habits, or thoughts that hinder our personal growth and negatively impact our overall well-being. These patterns often stem from deep-seated beliefs, traumas, or unresolved issues that we may carry from our past experiences. While they may provide a temporary sense of familiarity or comfort, they ultimately impede our ability to live a happy, productive, and fulfilling life.

Types of Destructive Patterns.

- **Relationship Patterns:** Unhealthy and toxic relationship dynamics marked by codependency, obsessiveness, or emotional manipulation.
- **Habits and Addictions:** Harmful habits such as substance abuse, excessive gambling, overeating, or compulsive spending that lead to detrimental consequences.
- **Negative Thought Patterns:** Persistent negative self-talk, self-doubt, catastrophizing, or excessive worrying that perpetuate an unhealthy mindset.
- **Procrastination and Self-Sabotage:** Repeatedly putting off tasks, making excuses, or undermining one's own success due to fear of failure or fear of success.
- **Victim Mentality:** Continuously perceiving oneself as a victim of circumstances, refusing to take ownership of one's actions and choices.

2. Recognizing Destructive Patterns.

Awareness is the first step towards ending destructive patterns. Without recognizing and acknowledging these patterns, it is challenging to change or break free from their grip.

A. Self-Reflection and Honest Evaluation.

- Cultivate self-awareness by reflecting on past and present patterns of behavior and thought.
- Engage in self-reflection exercises like journaling or mindfulness practices to gain clarity on underlying emotions, triggers, and beliefs.
- Seek feedback from trusted individuals who can provide an objective perspective on our behaviors and patterns.

B. Identifying Triggers and Patterns.

- Pay attention to recurring situations, emotions, or thoughts that lead to self-destructive behaviors.
- Identify patterns that emerge when faced with difficult or uncomfortable circumstances.
- Explore the root causes of these patterns, such as traumas, fears, or limiting beliefs.

3. Breaking Free from Destructive Patterns.

Once destructive patterns are recognized, it is crucial to develop strategies to end them and replace them with healthier alternatives.

A. Seeking Professional Help and Support.

- Consult with therapists, counselors, or life coaches who can provide guidance and insight into the underlying causes of destructive patterns.

- Engage in therapy or support groups to gain coping mechanisms, tools, and a supportive community during the journey of pattern transformation.

B. Embracing Self-Compassion and Positive Reinforcement.

- Practice self-compassion and understand that patterns develop as coping mechanisms rooted in pain or past experiences.
- Celebrate small victories and reinforce positive behaviors through self-reward systems.
- Surround ourselves with positive and supportive individuals who encourage growth and personal development.

C. Establishing New Habits and Behaviors.

- Replace destructive behaviors with healthier alternatives that align with personal values, goals, and desires.
- Develop new coping mechanisms through practices such as mindfulness, meditation, or taking up hobbies that promote personal growth.
- Create a structured routine and track progress to ensure consistency in adopting new habits.

4. Maintaining Progress and Sustaining Change.

Ending destructive patterns is an ongoing process that requires dedication, patience, and continued effort.

A. Building Resilience and Emotional Intelligence.

- Enhance emotional intelligence to understand and regulate emotions effectively.
- Cultivate resilience to bounce back from setbacks or relapses and stay committed to positive change.

B. Practicing Mindfulness and Self-Reflection.

- Utilize mindfulness techniques to stay present and aware of one's thoughts, feelings, and behaviors.
- Regularly engage in self-reflection exercises to evaluate progress, identify potential triggers, and refine strategies for personal growth.

Tips for Recognizing and Ending Destructive Patterns.

1. **Be honest with yourself:** Admit that you have destructive patterns that need to be addressed.
2. **Observe your behavior:** Take a step back and observe your actions and reactions in different situations.
3. **Identify your triggers:** Figure out what sets off your destructive patterns and why.
4. **Get support:** Seek the help of friends, family or a therapist to help you work through your patterns.
5. **Practice self-care:** Take care of yourself physically, emotionally and mentally.
6. **Keep a journal:** Write down your thoughts and feelings to better understand your destructive patterns.

7. **Set healthy boundaries:** Identify the situations and people that contribute to your destructive patterns and set boundaries.

8. **Break the cycle:** Make a conscious effort to change your behavior and response to triggers.

9. **Replace destructive habits with positive ones:** Find healthy ways to cope with stress and difficult situations.

10. **Celebrate your progress:** Recognize and celebrate your successes and progress along the way.

Benefits of Ending Destructive Patterns.

1. **Improved mental health:** Reducing destructive patterns can improve your overall mental health.

2. **Better relationships:** Addressing destructive patterns can lead to healthier relationships.

3. **Greater self-awareness:** Learning to recognize destructive patterns can lead to better self-awareness.

4. **More control:** Breaking destructive patterns can empower you with a greater sense of control over your life.

5. **Increased happiness:** Achieving healthier habits and relationships can lead to greater happiness.

6. **Better physical health:** Reducing stress and anxiety can have a positive impact on physical health.

7. **Improved productivity:** Breaking destructive patterns can increase productivity and enhance focus.

8. **Better decision-making:** Eliminating destructive patterns can lead to better decision-making.

9. **Greater self-esteem:** Addressing destructive patterns can boost self-esteem and confidence.

10. **Reduced regret:** Letting go of self-destructive patterns can reduce feelings of regret for past actions.

Functions of Recognizing and Ending Destructive Patterns.

1. **Developing healthy coping skills:** Breaking destructive patterns involves developing healthy coping mechanisms.

2. **Enhancing personal growth:** Addressing destructive patterns can promote personal growth and development.

3. **Creating a more positive outlook:** Focusing on positive habits and relationships can create a more positive outlook on life.

4. **Strengthening resilience:** Acknowledging and overcoming destructive patterns can strengthen resilience and the ability to bounce back from setbacks.

5. **Improving social skills:** Addressing destructive patterns can improve communication and social skills.

6. **Resolving inner conflicts:** Addressing destructive patterns can lead to resolution of inner conflicts.

7. **Establishing healthy boundaries:** Setting healthy boundaries is an important function of ending destructive patterns.

8. **Developing self-awareness:** Breaking destructive patterns requires developing self-awareness.

9. **Cultivating emotional intelligence:** Addressing destructive patterns can enhance emotional intelligence.

10. **Improving overall well-being:** Addressing destructive patterns can lead to improved overall well-being and quality of life.

Techniques to Recognize and End Destructive Patterns.

1. **Practice self-awareness:** Be mindful of your thoughts, emotions, and behaviour, and how they may contribute to negative patterns.
2. **Keep a journal:** Writing down your thoughts and experiences can help you identify patterns and triggers.
3. **Seek feedback:** Get feedback from trusted friends or family members who can provide an objective perspective.
4. **Use positive affirmations:** Affirmations can help reprogram your mind and break unhelpful patterns.
5. **Practice self-care:** Take care of yourself physically, mentally, and emotionally.
6. **Set boundaries:** Say no when you need to and establish clear boundaries with others.
7. **Challenge negative self-talk:** Recognize when negative self-talk is happening and counter it with positive affirmations or facts.
8. **Create a plan of action:** Identify steps you can take to break negative patterns and create positive ones.
9. **Practice mindfulness:** Be present in the moment and focus on your senses.
10. **Seek professional help:** Talk to a therapist or counselor if you need additional support.

Factors that Contribute to Destructive Patterns.

1. **Trauma:** Past experiences can have a profound impact on our thoughts, behaviour, and emotions.
2. **Genetics:** There may be a genetic component to certain patterns such as addiction or anxiety.
3. **Environment:** The people and situations around us can have a significant impact on our behavior.
4. **Lack of self-awareness:** Without an understanding of our own patterns, it can be difficult to break them.
5. **Learned behaviour:** We may learn destructive patterns from others or from our environment.
6. **Unaddressed mental health issues:** Mental health conditions can contribute to negative patterns.
7. **Lack of support:** Without a supportive network, it can be challenging to break destructive patterns.
8. **Stress:** High levels of stress can contribute to emotional instability and negative patterns.
9. **Low self-esteem:** A negative self-image can lead to destructive patterns.
10. **Lack of direction:** Without clear goals or purpose, it can be easy to fall into destructive patterns.

Causes of Destructive Patterns.

1. **Addiction:** Substance abuse or behavioural addiction can lead to destructive patterns.

2. **Codependency:** A pattern of depending on others can lead to neglecting one's own needs.

3. **Perfectionism:** A drive for perfection can lead to harsh self-criticism and stress.

4. **Control issues:** A need for control can lead to obsessiveness and anxiety.

5. **Avoidance:** Avoiding problems or difficult situations can lead to unresolved issues.

6. **Negative self-talk:** Internal criticism can lead to low self-esteem and stagnation.

7. **Procrastination:** Putting things off can lead to stress and missed opportunities.

8. **Impulsivity:** Acting without thinking can lead to poor decision-making and consequences.

9. **Insecurity:** A lack of confidence can lead to seeking validation from others.

10. **Self-sabotage:** A pattern of undermining one's own success or well-being can lead to negative outcomes.

Importance of Recognizing and Ending Destructive Patterns.

1. **Improves Mental Health:** When you recognize and end destructive patterns, you improve your mental health. You no longer have to deal with the negative emotions, anxiety, or depression that were brought on by your destructive behaviors.

2. **Enhances Relationships:** Destructive patterns within relationships can cause a lot of damage. By recognizing and

ending them, relationships can be enhanced, communication improved, and trust restored.

3. **Provides Self-Reflection:** When you recognize and end destructive patterns in your life, you are forced to look at your own behavior and reflect on why you may have been engaging in those behaviors.

4. **Increases Self-Awareness:** Ending destructive patterns in your life requires a heightened level of self-awareness. By doing so, you learn more about yourself and your motivations.

5. **Boosts Self-Esteem:** Whenever you break a bad habit or quit a destructive behavior, you feel proud of yourself for being able to change. This can boost your self-esteem and make you feel more confident.

6. **Clears Mind of Negativity:** Continuously engaging in destructive patterns can make your mind cluttered with negative thoughts. By ending those patterns, you clear your mind of that negativity and allow positive thoughts to take over.

7. **Creates Healthier Coping Mechanisms:** Frequently engaging in destructive behaviors can lead to unhealthy coping mechanisms. By ending those patterns, you create healthier ways of coping.

8. **Aids in Substance Abuse Recovery:** Recognizing and ending destructive patterns are a necessary step in substance abuse recovery. It allows addicts to let go of unhealthy habits and behaviors and create a new, healthier life.

9. **Improves Life Satisfaction:** Ending destructive patterns can lead to greater satisfaction in all aspects of your life. You may feel happier, more fulfilled, and more content.

10. **Gives You Control Over Your Life:** Engaging in destructive patterns can make you feel out of control. Ending those patterns put you back in charge of your life and your decisions.

Qualities That Aid in Recognizing and Ending Destructive Patterns.

1. Self-awareness.
2. Honesty.
3. Willingness to change
4. Open-mindedness.
5. Patience.
6. Persistence.
7. Acceptance.
8. Self-compassion.
9. Forgiveness.
10. Self-discipline.

Frameworks for Recognizing and Ending Destructive Patterns.

1. **Self-reflection:** take time to reflect on what triggers your destructive patterns.
2. **Journaling:** write down your thoughts and actions to understand patterns.

3. **Mindfulness:** Be present and observant of your thoughts and feelings.

4. **Cognitive Behavioral Therapy:** A therapeutic approach to changing thought patterns.

5. **Support groups:** Seek out others with similar struggles for support and accountability.

6. **Healthy habits:** Practice healthy habits to replace the destructive ones.

7. **Time management:** Organize your time to minimize stress.

8. **Motivation:** Find what motivates you to change and keep going.

9. **Professional help:** Seek out a therapist to help you recognize patterns and develop healthier habits.

10. **Gratitude:** Focus on what you are grateful for and cultivate an optimistic outlook on life.

Advantages or positive aspects of recognizing and ending destructive patterns.

1. **Self-awareness:** Identifying destructive patterns allows us to gain a deeper understanding of ourselves, our behaviors, and their impact on our lives.

2. **Personal growth:** By ending destructive patterns, we create opportunities for personal growth and development, leading to a more fulfilling and meaningful life.

3. **Improved well-being:** Breaking free from destructive patterns can positively impact our mental, emotional, and physical well-being, promoting overall health and happiness.

4. **Enhanced relationships:** Recognizing and addressing destructive patterns can improve our relationships by fostering healthier interactions and communication with others.

5. **Empowerment:** Ending destructive patterns empowers us to take control of our lives and make choices that align with our values, aspirations, and true selves.

6. **Increased productivity:** Eliminating self-sabotaging behaviors allows us to focus our energy and resources on activities that contribute to our goals and ambitions, leading to increased productivity.

7. **Better decision-making:** By recognizing and ending destructive patterns, we can develop better decision-making skills, enabling us to make choices that align with our long-term well-being and values.

8. **Improved self-esteem:** Breaking free from destructive patterns can enhance our self-esteem and self-worth, enabling us to believe in ourselves and our ability to create positive change.

9. **Resilience:** Recognizing and overcoming destructive patterns strengthens our resilience, equipping us with the tools to navigate challenges and setbacks more effectively.

10. **Positive role modeling:** By ending destructive patterns, we become positive role models for others, inspiring them to embark on their own journey of self-improvement and growth.

Disadvantages or potential obstacles of ending destructive patterns.

1. **Emotional discomfort:** Facing and addressing destructive patterns often involves emotional discomfort as we confront long-standing beliefs, fears, or traumas.

2. **Resistance to change:** Our mind and habits might resist change, making it challenging to overcome ingrained destructive patterns.

3. **Reliance on familiar coping mechanisms:** Breaking free from destructive patterns may require finding new healthy coping mechanisms, which can be daunting and uncomfortable.

4. **Fear of the unknown:** Embarking on personal growth and change involves stepping into the unknown, which can be unsettling and anxiety-inducing.

5. **Temporary setbacks:** Overcoming destructive patterns may involve setbacks or relapses along the way, which can hinder progress and be discouraging.

6. **Need for external support:** Recognizing and ending destructive patterns might require seeking help from therapists, support groups, or mentors, which can involve additional investment of time, effort, or resources.

7. **Challenging relationships:** Addressing our destructive patterns can sometimes lead to shifts in relationships, as we may outgrow certain dynamics or need to set healthier boundaries.

8. **Patience and persistence:** Ending destructive patterns is not an overnight process; it requires patience, resilience, and a commitment to long-term growth.

9. **Uncomfortable self-reflection:** The process of recognizing our destructive patterns often involves deep self-reflection, uncovering uncomfortable truths, and facing our own flaws and vulnerabilities.

10. **Potential resistance from others:** Some people around us might resist or feel uncomfortable with our personal growth journey, which can introduce complexities in our relationships.

Chapter 7: The Superhuman Strength of Optimism.

Optimism, defined as a positive outlook on life and the belief that favorable outcomes can be achieved, is a powerful mindset that has the ability to transform individuals, communities, and even the world. It is often described as a superhuman strength due to its ability to overcome challenges, inspire resilience, and create a harmonious environment. In this essay, we will explore the profound impact of optimism by examining its benefits, advantages, and positive consequences, while also considering its limitations and potential drawbacks.

Functions of Recognizing and Ending Destructive Patterns.

1. **Personal growth:** By recognizing destructive patterns, you open yourself to self-awareness and the opportunity for personal development.

2. **Improved relationships:** Ending destructive patterns allows you to build healthier and more fulfilling relationships with others.

3. **Emotional well-being:** Breaking free from destructive habits can lead to increased emotional stability and a greater sense of inner peace.

4. **Enhanced decision-making:** Recognizing destructive patterns allows you to make more informed and positive choices in various aspects of your life.

5. **Increased self-esteem:** Letting go of self-destructive behaviors can boost your self-confidence and improve your overall self-image.

6. **Improved productivity:** Breaking free from destructive patterns can help you regain focus and contribute to increased productivity in your personal and professional life.

7. **Better physical health:** Ending destructive habits like excessive stress or substance abuse can have positive effects on your physical well-being.

8. **Greater life satisfaction:** Letting go of destructive patterns allows you to experience a greater sense of contentment and fulfillment in life.

9. **Improved problem-solving skills:** Recognizing destructive patterns helps you develop resilience and effective strategies for overcoming challenges.

10. **Authenticity:** Letting go of destructive habits allows you to be true to yourself and live a more authentic and fulfilling life.

Benefits of Cultivating the Superhuman Strength of Optimism.

1. **Practice gratitude:** Cultivating optimism involves appreciating the positive aspects of your life and expressing gratitude for them.
2. **Positive affirmations:** Use positive self-talk and affirmations to reframe negative thoughts and beliefs into more optimistic ones.
3. **Surround yourself with positivity:** Surrounding yourself with positive people and environments can help reinforce an optimistic mindset.
4. **Focus on solutions:** Instead of dwelling on problems, concentrate on finding solutions and taking action to overcome challenges.
5. **Embrace failures as learning opportunities:** Maintain an optimistic outlook by seeing failures as stepping stones towards growth and success.
6. **Visualization:** Visualize your goals and desired outcomes, allowing yourself to believe in the possibility of achieving them.
7. **Self-care:** Prioritize self-care activities that promote overall well-being, such as exercise, adequate rest, and healthy habits.
8. **Flexible thinking:** Foster a mindset of adaptability and open-mindedness, enabling you to see alternative perspectives and possibilities.

9. **Develop resilience:** Cultivating optimism involves building resilience and bouncing back from setbacks with a positive attitude.

10. **Spread positivity:** Share kindness and positivity with others, as it not only enhances their lives but also reinforces your own optimistic mindset.

The Pros of Optimism.

1. **Improved Mental Health:** Optimism has been linked to reduced stress levels, better coping mechanisms, and increased psychological well-being. It allows individuals to navigate through difficulties with a more positive mindset, enhancing resilience and overall mental health.

2. **Physical Well-being:** Optimistic people tend to lead healthier lifestyles, including regular exercise, balanced diets, and adequate sleep. This optimistic approach is associated with lower risks of chronic diseases and promotes longevity.

3. **Enhanced Relationships:** Optimistic individuals exude positive energy and are more likely to attract and maintain fulfilling relationships. Their hopeful outlook fosters empathy, communication, and connection, contributing to a harmonious social environment.

4. **Motivation and Achievement:** Optimism acts as a catalyst for personal growth and achievement. Optimistic individuals set ambitious goals, maintain a belief in their abilities, and persevere through challenges, thus increasing their chances of success.

5. **Inspires Resilience:** Optimism enables individuals to bounce back from setbacks and traumatic experiences. It empowers them to view failures as temporary and learn from their mistakes, leading to personal growth and resilience.

6. **Problem-Solving and Creativity:** An optimistic mindset fuels innovative thinking, encourages out-of-the-box problem solving, and promotes creativity. It allows individuals to approach challenges with enthusiasm, finding constructive solutions.

7. **Leadership Qualities:** Optimistic individuals possess qualities desired in effective leaders. Their positive outlook inspires trust, motivates teams, and fosters a supportive work environment, resulting in increased productivity and success.

8. **Strengthened Immune System:** Studies have shown that optimists have a stronger immune response, better resistance to illnesses, and faster recovery rates, highlighting the physical benefits of optimism.

9. **Increased Happiness and Well-being:** Optimism is closely associated with higher levels of life satisfaction and overall happiness. It allows individuals to appreciate the present, find joy in everyday experiences, and cultivate a sense of purpose.

10. **Social and Community Impact:** Optimistic individuals have the power to positively influence their social networks and communities. Their hopeful and proactive approach inspires others to take action, contributing to collective growth and development.

The Cons of Optimism.

1. **Unrealistic Expectations:** Optimism, when taken to an extreme, may lead to unrealistic expectations and a detachment from reality. This can result in disappointment and discouragement when faced with genuine challenges or setbacks.

2. **Ignoring Potential Risks:** Overly optimistic individuals may overlook potential risks or downplay negative circumstances, leading to poor decision-making and an underestimation of potential consequences.

3. **Lack of Preparedness:** While optimism can inspire confidence and enthusiasm, it may also result in a lack of preparedness for potential obstacles or future uncertainties. This could lead to unanticipated difficulties and setbacks.

4. **Suppression of Negative Emotions:** Optimism can sometimes discourage individuals from acknowledging and addressing negative emotions such as sadness, anger, or fear. This may prevent healthy emotional processing and hinder personal growth.

5. **Disregard for Realistic Alternatives:** In certain situations, optimism may lead to a dismissal of realistic alternatives, limiting critical evaluation and potentially missing out on better options or innovative solutions.

6. **Disruption of Healthy Boundaries:** In extreme cases, optimism can lead individuals to tolerate negative situations or relationships for longer periods, with the belief that things

will eventually improve. This may lead to a compromise of personal boundaries and well-being.

7. **Resistance to Change:** Optimistic individuals may resist or overlook the need for necessary changes or adjustments, as they may perceive them as unnecessary or detrimental to their positive outcomes.

8. **Potential for Naivety:** Excessive optimism can make individuals vulnerable to exploitation or manipulation by disregarding warning signs or red flags, leading to poor judgment and decision-making.

9. **Cultural and Contextual Factors:** Optimism may be influenced by cultural and contextual factors, with some societies or environments fostering unrealistic expectations or stifling pessimism for the sake of conformity.

10. **Potential Disruption of Realism and Critical Thinking:** While optimism is a valuable mindset, too much emphasis on positive outcomes may undermine the importance of critical thinking and realistic assessment of situations.

Chapter 8: The Power of Collaboration.

Nobody Can Accomplish Anything Alone.

In a world that glorifies individual achievements and champions the concept of self-reliance, it is easy to overlook the profound truth that nobody can accomplish anything alone. Success, be it in personal or professional endeavors, is often the result of collaboration, synergy, and collective effort. This essay aims to shed light on the inherent significance of collaboration by examining the ways it can manifest as a driving force for achieving greatness. By exploring diverse perspectives, examples, and scientific research, we will uncover the limitations of individualism and highlight the numerous benefits that collaboration brings to both individuals and society as a whole.

1. Shared Knowledge and Expertise.

One of the key advantages of collaboration is the accumulation and sharing of knowledge and expertise. When individuals come together, they bring with them a diverse range of experiences, skills, and perspectives. By pooling their collective knowledge, they form a rich reservoir of ideas and solutions that surpasses what any single person could achieve on their own. This collaboration allows for more comprehensive problem-solving and innovation.

2. Strength in Numbers.

Collaboration harnesses the power of numbers, making it possible to tackle complex challenges that might otherwise overwhelm an individual. From large-scale community projects to cutting-edge scientific research, achieving significant milestones often requires the combined efforts and resources of many individuals. By banding together, groups can amplify their impact, overcome obstacles, and achieve exponential growth.

3. Support and Motivation.

Undertaking important tasks alone can be emotionally draining and demotivating, amplifying the risk of burnout and discouragement. Collaboration provides a support system that helps individuals navigate through setbacks, maintain focus, and stay motivated. Through encouragement, praise, and shared determination, collaborators can create a positive environment that fosters resilience and achievement.

4. Complementary Skill Sets.

Each person possesses a unique set of skills, strengths, and weaknesses. Collaboration enables individuals to combine their diverse skill sets, fortifying their collective abilities and compensating for individual limitations. By leveraging the strengths of others, individuals can enhance their own performance and achieve outcomes that surpass their individual potentials.

5. Innovation and Creativity.

Through collaboration, ideas converge, collide, and evolve. Interactions between individuals with distinct perspectives often spark innovation and creative solutions. Collaborative environments encourage open dialogue, constructive criticism, and brainstorming sessions where ideas flourish. This dynamic process nurtures a culture of innovation that leads to breakthroughs and disruptive solutions.

6. Increased Efficiency and Productivity.

When individuals work in isolation, duplication of effort and wastage of resources are common pitfalls. Collaboration promotes efficiency by dividing tasks, sharing responsibilities, and streamlining processes. By capitalizing on the strengths of each team member, collaboration fosters productivity, enabling goals to be achieved in a shorter timeframe and with higher quality outcomes.

7. Learning and Personal Growth.

Collaboration provides a fertile ground for personal growth and development. When individuals work alongside their peers, they have the opportunity to observe and learn from others' experiences, gain new skills, and expand their own knowledge. Through collaboration, individuals are exposed to diverse perspectives, resulting in personal growth, increased adaptability, and a broader understanding of the world.

8. Enhanced Problem-Solving.

Complex challenges often require multifaceted solutions that stem from a deep analysis of the problem at hand. Collaboration allows for collective problem-solving, inviting different viewpoints and insights into the discussion. By combining various perspectives, collaborators can generate creative alternatives and evaluate potential solutions more comprehensively, leading to more effective problem-solving outcomes.

9. Building Social Connections.

Collaboration nurtures connections and fosters social bonds. By working collaboratively, individuals establish relationships based on trust, respect, and shared goals. These connections contribute to a stronger sense of belonging, fostering a supportive and cohesive environment. Furthermore, these social ties can extend beyond the immediate project, resulting in future opportunities and a robust professional network.

10. Collective Impact and Social Change.

Some of the greatest achievements in history have been the result of collaborative efforts aimed at social change. From civil rights movements to environmental activism, collaboration has been a driving force in creating lasting positive impact. The ability to mobilize and unite individuals around a shared purpose allows for the creation of movements that can challenge the status quo, advocate for justice, and effect meaningful change.

Tips of the Power of Collaboration.

1. **Foster Open Communication:** Encourage team members to express their ideas, concerns, and suggestions openly.

2. **Embrace Diverse Perspectives:** Value and incorporate different viewpoints, as it leads to more creative and comprehensive solutions.

3. **Establish Clear Goals:** Clearly define the objectives, ensuring everyone is aligned and understands what needs to be accomplished.

4. **Delegate Tasks:** Distribute responsibilities according to individual strengths and expertise, promoting efficiency and accountability.

5. **Encourage Brainstorming:** Encourage team members to engage in brainstorming sessions to generate innovative ideas and solutions.

6. **Foster a Supportive Environment:** Create a workplace culture that supports collaboration, where individuals feel safe to contribute and take risks.

7. **Promote Active Listening:** Encourage attentive listening to understand others' perspectives fully and foster collaboration.

8. **Resolve Conflict Effectively:** Develop conflict resolution strategies to address disagreements constructively and maintain a harmonious working environment.

9. **Establish Clear Roles and Responsibilities:** Clearly outline each team member's role, ensuring clarity and minimizing confusion.

10. **Celebrate Successes:** Recognize and appreciate collaborative achievements, reinforcing the importance of working together.

Benefits of the Power of Collaboration.

1. **Increased Efficiency:** Collaboration allows for division of labor and sharing of responsibilities, leading to greater efficiency in completing tasks.
2. **Enhanced Problem Solving:** Combining diverse perspectives and expertise enables more effective problem-solving through a collective intellect.
3. **Improved Innovation:** Collaboration sparks creativity, as individuals bring unique ideas and insights to the table, fostering innovation.
4. **Strengthened Relationships:** Working together towards common goals fosters stronger bonds among team members, enhancing overall relationships.
5. **Higher Morale:** Collaboration promotes a sense of inclusion, involvement, and shared purpose, which boosts morale and employee satisfaction.
6. **Expanded Knowledge:** By collaborating with others, individuals can tap into a broader pool of expertise and knowledge, expanding their own understanding.
7. **Faster Decision Making:** Collaborative environments facilitate faster decision-making processes as multiple perspectives and solutions are considered.

8. **Enhanced Adaptability:** Collaboration equips teams with the ability to adapt to changes more effectively, particularly in complex or uncertain situations.

9. **Increased Accountability:** Collaboration encourages a sense of collective responsibility, leading to increased individual accountability towards shared goals.

10. **Overall Success:** Utilizing the power of collaboration increases the likelihood of achieving successful outcomes, surpassing what could be accomplished individually.

Functions of the Power of Collaboration.

1. **Knowledge Sharing:** Collaboration facilitates the sharing of ideas, information, and expertise among team members.

2. **Task Coordination:** Collaboration allows for effective coordination and allocation of tasks to ensure efficient completion.

3. **Conflict Resolution:** Collaborative efforts help in resolving conflicts or differences in opinions through open discussion and mutual understanding.

4. **Brainstorming:** Collaboration encourages collective brainstorming sessions to generate a wide range of ideas and solutions.

5. **Decision Making:** Collaborative decision-making processes involve collective input, analysis, and consensus-building to reach optimal solutions.

6. **Resource Utilization:** Collaborative efforts help in pooling resources, including skills, expertise, and tools, for more efficient resource utilization.

7. **Feedback Exchange:** Collaboration includes providing and receiving constructive feedback, promoting continuous improvement and growth.

8. **Support and Mentorship:** Collaboration fosters a supportive environment where team members can provide guidance and mentorship to one another.

9. **Learning and Development:** Collaborative settings provide opportunities for individuals to learn from each other, fostering personal and professional growth.

10. **Problem Solving:** Collaboration enables teams to tackle complex problems by leveraging diverse perspectives, generating innovative solutions.

Techniques of the Power of Collaboration.

1. **Brainstorming:** Collaborative brainstorming sessions allow for the generation of diverse ideas and perspectives.

2. **Active listening:** Being attentive and genuinely listening to others fosters effective communication and understanding within a collaborative setting.

3. **Division of labor:** Assigning specific tasks and responsibilities based on individual strengths and expertise promotes efficiency and productivity.

4. **Regular communication:** Maintaining open lines of communication ensures that all team members stay informed, aligned, and motivated.

5. **Constructive feedback:** Offering feedback in a respectful and constructive manner enables continuous improvement and growth.

6. **Flexibility and compromise:** Being open to alternative viewpoints and finding middle ground through compromise encourages collaboration and avoids conflicts.

7. **Leveraging technology:** Utilizing collaborative tools and platforms allows team members to work together effectively, regardless of physical location.

8. **Clear goal-setting:** Establishing and communicating clear goals ensures that everyone understands the collective purpose and works towards it.

9. **Celebrate achievements:** Recognizing and celebrating milestones and achievements boosts team morale and motivation.

10. **Reflection and learning:** Regularly reflecting on collaborative efforts and learning from both successes and failures helps refine future collaborative endeavors.

Factors of the Power of Collaboration.

1. **Diversity:** Collaborating with individuals from different backgrounds, experiences, and expertise brings a broader range of ideas and perspectives.

2. **Creativity:** Collaboration stimulates creativity and encourages innovative solutions by pooling together unique insights and approaches.

3. **Improved decision-making:** Collective decision-making allows for a more comprehensive evaluation of options and reduces the likelihood of biases.

4. **Enhanced problem-solving:** Combining diverse skills and knowledge enhances problem-solving capabilities, leading to more effective solutions.

5. **Increased efficiency:** Collaboration allows tasks to be shared, leading to greater efficiency and faster completion of projects.

6. **Mutual support:** Collaborative environments offer a support system where team members can provide assistance and encouragement to one another.

7. **Learning opportunities:** Collaboration promotes continuous learning as team members share knowledge and skills with each other.

8. **Task specialization:** In collaborative settings, individuals can focus on tasks that align with their strengths, resulting in higher-quality outputs.

9. **Networking:** Collaborative projects provide opportunities to build connections and expand professional networks.

10. **Adaptability:** Collaboration fosters a culture of adaptability, enabling teams to respond and adjust to changing circumstances and emerging challenges.

Causes of the Power of Collaboration.

1. **Interdependence:** Many tasks require the skills, knowledge, and efforts of multiple individuals, necessitating collaboration.

2. **Complexity:** Complex problems often require diverse perspectives and expertise that collaboration can offer.

3. **Scale and scope:** Large-scale projects necessitate collaboration to effectively manage the workload and resources.

4. **Time constraints:** Collaboration can accelerate the progress of projects by allowing tasks to be divided among team members.

5. **Organizational culture:** Companies with a collaborative culture tend to foster teamwork and actively promote collaboration.

6. **Trust and relationship-building:** Collaboration relies on trust and positive relationships among team members to succeed.

7. **External factors:** Market shifts, changing customer demands, or industry disruptions can encourage collaborative efforts to adapt and survive.

8. **Shared objectives:** When individuals or organizations share common goals, collaboration becomes a means to achieve those objectives.

9. **Knowledge exchange:** Collaboration facilitates the sharing and transfer of knowledge, leading to collective growth and development.

10. **Recognition of limitations:** Acknowledging personal or organizational limitations can prompt collaboration with others who possess complementary skills or resources.

Importance of Collaboration.

1. **Achieving common goals:** Collaboration allows individuals with diverse skills and perspectives to work together towards a shared objective, increasing the likelihood of achieving success.

2. **Enhanced creativity and innovation:** Through collaboration, different ideas are brought together, fostering creativity and the ability to generate innovative solutions.

3. **Exchange of knowledge and learning:** Collaborative environments encourage knowledge-sharing, enabling individuals to learn from each other's expertise and experiences.

4. **Increased efficiency:** By leveraging the strengths of each team member, collaboration can lead to streamlined processes and improved efficiency in completing tasks.

5. **Building strong relationships:** Collaboration strengthens interpersonal relationships, fostering trust, respect, and effective communication among team members.

6. **Problem-solving capabilities:** Collaborative efforts allow for collective problem-solving, as multiple perspectives and insights can be combined to find optimal solutions.

7. **Sharing the workload:** Collaboration helps distribute responsibilities, preventing individuals from becoming overwhelmed and ensuring a fair distribution of tasks.

8. **Increased adaptability:** Collaborative teams are often more adaptable to change, as they can tap into diverse perspectives when responding to new challenges or unforeseen circumstances.

9. **Enhancing personal growth:** Through collaboration, individuals can develop new skills, expand their knowledge, and improve their own professional growth.

10. **Promoting a positive work culture:** Collaboration fosters a positive work atmosphere characterized by teamwork, mutual support, and camaraderie.

Qualities that Foster Collaboration.

1. **Active listening:** Being attentive any receptive to others' ideas and perspectives, allowing for effective communication and understanding.

2. **Respect for diverse viewpoints:** Valuing and appreciating different opinions, backgrounds, and experiences within the collaborative process.

3. **Open-mindedness:** Being receptive to new ideas, embracing change, and maintaining flexibility in thinking.

4. **Effective communication:** Clearly expressing thoughts, actively engaging in discussions, and providing feedback to ensure seamless information flow.

5. **Trust and transparency:** Building trust among team members through open and honest communication, fostering a safe and supportive environment.

6. **Conflict resolution skills:** Managing conflicts constructively, seeking compromise, and finding resolutions that benefit everyone involved.

7. **Accountability:** Taking ownership of assigned tasks and delivering on commitments made to the team.

8. **Emotional intelligence:** Understanding and managing emotions, both one's own and others', to foster positive and productive interactions.

9. **Empathy:** Showing empathy towards colleagues' perspectives, challenges, and feelings, and considering their needs in decision-making processes.

10. **Adaptability:** Being willing to embrace change, adjust plans, and make necessary shifts in direction to accommodate the collaborative process.

Framework for Effective Collaboration.

1. **Clearly defined purpose and goals:** Establishing a common understanding of the purpose and desired outcomes of the collaboration effort.

2. **Roles and responsibilities:** Clearly defining the roles and responsibilities of each team member to ensure clarity and accountability.

3. **Regular communication channels:** Implementing effective communication channels, such as regular meetings, virtual

platforms, and shared documentation, to facilitate information exchange.

4. **Mutual trust and respect:** Creating an environment built on trust and respect, where individuals feel comfortable sharing ideas and feedback.

5. **Effective leadership:** Having strong leaders who can guide the collaborative process, facilitate discussions, and make timely decisions when required.

6. **Encouraging diverse participation:** Creating opportunities for active participation from all team members, ensuring that diverse perspectives are considered.

7. **Conflict management mechanisms:** Establishing protocols and processes for managing conflicts constructively, encouraging open dialogue and resolution.

8. **Clear decision-making procedures:** Defining decision-making procedures to ensure a structured approach in reaching consensus or making informed choices.

9. **Continuous evaluation and feedback:** Regularly assessing the progress and effectiveness of collaboration efforts, and providing constructive feedback to drive improvement.

10. **Celebrating achievements:** Acknowledging and celebrating milestones and achievements, motivating team members and reinforcing the value of collaboration.

Pros / Advantages of the Power of Collaboration.

1. **Personal Growth:** By recognizing and ending destructive patterns, you can experience significant personal growth and self-improvement.

2. **Improved Relationships:** Breaking free from destructive patterns allows you to cultivate healthier and more fulfilling relationships with others.

3. **Emotional Well-being:** Letting go of destructive patterns can lead to increased emotional well-being, helping you manage stress and anxiety more effectively.

4. **Enhanced Decision Making:** By overcoming destructive patterns, you can make better decisions based on clarity and rationality rather than being driven by negative impulses.

5. **Inner Peace:** Breaking free from destructive patterns can bring a sense of inner peace and contentment, allowing you to experience more joy and fulfillment in life.

6. **Increased Productivity:** When you eliminate destructive patterns, you can focus your energy and efforts in a more productive and efficient manner.

7. **Better Health:** Certain destructive patterns, such as unhealthy habits, can harm your physical well-being. Breaking free from them can improve your overall health.

8. **Enhanced Creativity:** Letting go of patterns that limit your thinking can unlock new levels of creativity and innovation.

9. **Improved Self-esteem:** Ending destructive patterns leads to a boost in self-confidence and self-esteem, as you gain control over your actions and choices.

10. **Greater Resilience:** Overcoming destructive patterns equips you with the resilience needed to face life's challenges with a positive mindset.

Cons / Challenges of the Power of Collaboration.

1. **Initial Discomfort:** Overcoming destructive patterns often involves stepping out of your comfort zone, which can be challenging and uncomfortable at first.

2. **Temptation to Relapse:** Destructive patterns can draw you back in through temptation or triggers, requiring ongoing vigilance and effort to prevent relapse.

3. **Resistance from Others:** Sometimes, people close to you might resist or have difficulty accepting the changes you are making, which can create tension or strain on relationships.

4. **Emotional Turmoil:** As you confront and address destructive patterns, it's possible to experience emotional turmoil or temporary setbacks.

5. **Loneliness and Isolation:** Ending certain destructive patterns might lead to distancing yourself from people or environments that perpetuate those patterns, which can result in temporary feelings of loneliness.

6. **Fear of the Unknown:** Letting go of familiar destructive patterns might create a fear of uncertainty and the unknown, making it challenging to embrace change.

7. **Patience and Persistence Required:** Breaking free from destructive patterns takes time and consistent effort; it may not happen overnight.

8. **Identifying Root Causes:** Identifying the underlying causes or triggers for your destructive patterns can be a complex and introspective process.

9. **Need for Support:** Overcoming destructive patterns often requires seeking support from trusted friends, family, or professionals, which can be challenging for some individuals.

10. **Personal Responsibility:** Recognizing and ending destructive patterns requires taking ownership of your actions and choices, which can be a demanding process.

Chapter 9: From Achievement to Importance.

Embracing a Paradigm Shift towards Meaningful Existence.

In today's fast-paced and achievement-oriented society, individuals often find themselves entrenched in a relentless pursuit of external success and recognition. While accomplishments and accolades undoubtedly play a role in personal growth, defining one's life solely based on achievements can lead to a shallow and unfulfilling existence. In this essay, we will explore the paradigm shift from a focus on achievement to embracing the importance of leading a meaningful life. We will discuss how prioritizing importance over achievement can lead to greater personal satisfaction, enriched relationships, and a positive impact on society.

1. The Pitfalls of Achievement-driven Mindsets.

- **Superficial Fulfillment:** An overemphasis on achievement often leads to superficial fulfillment, as external markers such as wealth, status, and material possessions become primary sources of happiness. This shallow sense of fulfillment can lead to a constant cycle of chasing more achievements without finding true contentment.

- **Neglected Personal Growth:** An achievement-driven mindset tends to overshadow the importance of personal growth and self-reflection. It places value solely on external validation, neglecting the internal journey necessary for self-improvement and self-actualization.

- **Strained Relationships:** Focusing excessively on achievements can strain personal relationships, as individuals may prioritize their ambitions over nurturing connections with loved ones. The relentless pursuit of success can create distance and hinder the development of meaningful bonds.

- **Burnout and Stress:** Constantly striving for achievements can result in burnout and chronic stress. The pressure to succeed can have detrimental effects on mental and physical well-being, leading to decreased overall satisfaction with life.

2. The Shift towards Emphasizing Importance.

- **Discovering Personal Values:** Shifting focus from achievement to importance involves identifying one's core values and aligning actions with those values. This introspective process allows individuals to live a life that is truly meaningful to them.

- **Cultivating Inner Satisfaction:** Embracing a mindset that prioritizes importance encourages individuals to find satisfaction in the journey rather than solely in the outcome.

It promotes self-acceptance, mindfulness, and an appreciation for life's simple pleasures.

- **Cultivating Authentic Relationships:** Placing importance on deep and authentic connections fosters healthier relationships. Giving time and attention to loved ones, friends, and community builds a support system and enhances overall well-being.
- **Promoting Well-being:** Shifting focus towards leading a life of importance promotes holistic well-being. It encourages individuals to prioritize self-care, mental health, and maintain a healthy work-life balance.

Tips for Embracing a Paradigm Shift towards Meaningful Existence.

1. **Reflect on your values:** Take time to identify and prioritize your core values. Understanding what truly matters to you will help shape your decisions and actions in alignment with your beliefs.

2. **Set meaningful goals:** Instead of pursuing goals solely based on external validation, set goals that are personally meaningful and contribute to your growth, fulfillment, and the betterment of others.

3. **Cultivate self-awareness:** Engage in practices such as meditation, journaling, or therapy to develop a deep understanding of yourself, your emotions, and your motivations. This will enable you to make conscious choices and lead a more authentic life.

4. **Foster positive relationships:** Surround yourself with individuals who share your values and inspire you to become the best version of yourself. Meaningful connections provide support, encouragement, and a sense of belonging.

5. **Embrace gratitude:** Practice gratitude regularly to shift your focus towards appreciating what you have rather than constantly striving for more. Gratitude cultivates contentment and a sense of abundance in the present moment.

6. **Engage in self-care:** Prioritize your well-being by taking care of your physical, emotional, and mental health. Regular exercise, adequate rest, nourishing food, and self-reflection activities contribute to a balanced and fulfilling life.

7. **Seek new experiences:** Step out of your comfort zone and embrace opportunities for growth and learning. Trying new things broadens your perspective, builds resilience, and deepens your understanding of the world.

8. **Give back to others:** Engaging in acts of kindness and service not only benefits those in need but also brings joy, fulfillment, and a profound sense of purpose to your own life.

9. **Live in alignment with your principles:** Make choices and actions consistent with your beliefs and values. Living authentically means embodying your principles in everyday life, regardless of external pressures or societal expectations.

10. **Practice mindfulness:** Cultivate mindfulness by being present and fully engaged in the present moment. Mindfulness helps enhance your focus, reduce stress, and increase your capacity for compassion and empathy.

Benefits of Embracing a Paradigm Shift towards Meaningful Existence.

1. **Increased overall life satisfaction:** Embracing a life of purpose and meaning fosters a sense of fulfillment and contentment, leading to higher levels of life satisfaction.

2. **Improved mental well-being:** By prioritizing what truly matters, you are likely to experience reduced stress, anxiety, and depression, promoting better mental health.

3. **Enhanced relationships:** Meaningful existence encourages nurturing and authentic connections, resulting in deeper and more fulfilling relationships with others.

4. **Greater resilience:** Embracing a paradigm shift allows you to build resilience and adaptability, enabling you to navigate life's challenges with strength and determination.

5. **Improved self-confidence:** Living in alignment with your values and goals boosts your self-confidence, empowering you to pursue your passions and overcome self-doubt.

6. **Sense of fulfillment:** A meaningful existence brings a profound sense of fulfillment derived from contributing to something larger than oneself, creating a lasting legacy.

7. **Increased motivation:** When driven by purpose and importance, you are more likely to stay motivated and persist in the face of setbacks, leading to greater achievements.

8. **Clarity of direction:** By embracing meaningful existence, you gain clarity in your purpose and find a clear direction for your life, leading to more focused and intentional actions.

9. **Enhanced personal growth:** Prioritizing meaning and significance supports continuous personal growth and development, unlocking your true potential.

10. **Positive impact on society:** By living a meaningful existence, you have the power to positively impact the world around you, inspiring others to embrace their own paradigm shift towards significance.

Functions of Embracing a Paradigm Shift towards Meaningful Existence.

1. **Provides a compass for decision-making:** Having clarity on your values and purpose guides your decision-making process, ensuring your choices align with what matters most to you.

2. **Shapes your identity:** Embracing a meaningful existence helps shape your sense of self, allowing you to discover and express your authentic identity.

3. **Fosters personal accountability:** By prioritizing meaning over achievement, you become more accountable for your actions, taking ownership of creating a fulfilling life.

4. **Inspires personal growth and development:** Embracing a paradigm shift towards significance encourages continuous growth, allowing you to continually evolve and become the best version of yourself.

5. **Serves as a source of motivation:** Living a life of purpose and importance provides intrinsic motivation, driving you to take action towards your goals and aspirations.

6. **Cultivates resilience and adaptability:** Prioritizing meaning fosters resilience, aiding in bouncing back from setbacks and adapting to changing circumstances.

7. **Deepens self-awareness:** By reflecting on your values and priorities, you develop a deeper understanding of yourself, enhancing self-awareness and self-compassion.

8. **Nurtures empathy and compassion:** A paradigm shift towards meaningful existence promotes empathy and compassion for others, leading to increased understanding and a desire to make a positive difference.

9. **Creates a sense of fulfillment:** Embracing importance and significance brings about a lasting sense of fulfillment that comes from making a meaningful impact on the world.

10. **Cultivates a legacy:** By living in alignment with your values and contributing to something larger than yourself, you create a legacy that extends beyond your own existence, leaving a positive impression on future generations.

Techniques to Embrace a Paradigm Shift towards Meaningful Existence.

1. **Mindfulness:** Cultivate present-moment awareness to fully engage with your life experiences and find meaning in them.

2. **Self-reflection:** Take time to reflect on your values, beliefs, and goals to align your actions with what truly matters to you.

3. **Gratitude:** Practice gratitude by acknowledging and appreciating the positive aspects of your life, fostering a sense of fulfillment.

4. **Simplify:** Streamline your life by decluttering your physical and mental space, allowing you to focus on what is truly important.

5. **Purposeful goal-setting:** Set meaningful and purpose-driven goals that align with your values, providing a sense of direction and fulfillment.

6. **Embrace personal growth:** Continuously seek opportunities for learning, self-improvement, and personal development, expanding your perspective and sense of purpose.

7. **Foster meaningful relationships:** Prioritize nurturing supportive connections and surround yourself with individuals who share your values and can contribute to your growth.

8. **Contribution and service:** Engage in acts of kindness and make a positive difference in the lives of others, recognizing the inherent value in serving others.

9. **Practice self-care:** Prioritize your well-being by taking care of your physical, emotional, and mental health, allowing you to show up fully for yourself and others.

10. **Embrace uncertainty:** Embrace the unknown and let go of the need for control, as life's uncertainties have the potential to lead to unexpected growth and meaning.

Factors Contributing to a Paradigm Shift towards Meaningful Existence.

1. **Self-awareness:** Being conscious of one's values, beliefs, and desires lays the foundation for seeking a more meaningful existence.
2. **Personal growth:** Actively pursuing self-improvement and embracing opportunities for growth opens new pathways to finding purpose.
3. **Shift in perspective:** Adopting a broader perspective and questioning societal norms and expectations can lead to questioning the pursuit of achievement versus the pursuit of importance.
4. **Reflective practices:** Engaging in practices like journaling, meditation, or therapy encourages introspection and self-discovery.
5. **Social support:** Surrounding oneself with like-minded individuals who value meaningful existence can provide a support system and reinforce the shift towards prioritizing importance.
6. **Life experiences:** Challenging life events or moments of crisis can prompt a reevaluation of priorities and lead to a paradigm shift.
7. **Connection to something greater:** Developing a sense of connection to something greater than oneself, such as nature, spirituality, or a purpose-driven cause, can infuse life with meaning.

8. **Self-acceptance:** Learning to accept oneself, including strengths and flaws, enables a more authentic and fulfilling existence.

9. **Aligning actions with values:** Intentionally living in a way that aligns with personal values fosters a sense of purpose and meaning.

10. **Embracing vulnerability:** Allowing oneself to be vulnerable and open to uncertainty can lead to growth and the discovery of new opportunities for a meaningful existence.

Causes Driving a Paradigm Shift towards Meaningful Existence.

1. **Cultural shifts:** Societal movements and changes that challenge the status quo can influence individuals to reconsider the pursuit of achievement and prioritize meaningful experiences.

2. **Burnout and dissatisfaction:** Increasing rates of burnout and dissatisfaction with conventional success metrics can prompt individuals to seek a more purposeful existence.

3. **Existential questioning:** Philosophical inquiry, contemplation of mortality, or existential crises can lead to a quest for a more meaningful and fulfilling life.

4. **Desire for authentic connections:** The longing for deeper, more authentic connections with oneself and others can drive individuals towards prioritizing importance over achievement.

5. **Global challenges:** Rising awareness of global issues and the need for collective action can motivate individuals to shift

their focus towards making a positive impact and finding meaning through purpose-driven pursuits.

6. **Personal growth journeys:** Individuals who have undergone personal growth journeys, such as therapy or self-help practices, may experience a shift in values and priorities towards a more meaningful existence.

7. **Inspirational figures:** Role models and influencers who embody a meaningful existence can inspire others to reassess their own life choices and values.

8. **The pursuit of well-being:** Recognizing the limitations of material success in fostering long-term happiness and well-being can prompt individuals to seek meaning beyond achievements.

9. **Authenticity and identity exploration:** Engaging in self-exploration and uncovering one's authentic self can lead to a desire for a more meaningful existence that aligns with personal values and aspirations.

10. **Reflection on legacy:** Contemplating the legacy one wants to leave behind can prompt a shift towards prioritizing meaningful experiences and contributions over mere accomplishments.

Importance of embracing this paradigm shift.

1. **Purpose:** Understanding the importance of having a clear purpose in life provides us with direction and a sense of fulfillment.

2. **Connection:** Recognizing the significance of healthy relationships and fostering meaningful connections with others supports our overall well-being.

3. **Growth:** Embracing the importance of personal growth and continuous learning enables us to expand our horizons and reach our full potential.

4. **Authenticity:** Embodying our true selves and living in alignment with our values cultivates a sense of purpose and authenticity.

5. **Gratitude:** Acknowledging and appreciating the importance of gratitude allows us to find joy and contentment in life's simplest moments.

6. **Mindfulness:** Being present in the moment and practicing mindfulness helps us to better understand ourselves and our surroundings, leading to a more meaningful experience.

7. **Contribution:** Recognizing the significance of giving back to our communities and making a positive impact on the world around us brings a deep sense of purpose.

8. **Balance:** Understanding the importance of creating a balanced lifestyle ensures that we prioritize our well-being and avoid burnout.

9. **Resilience:** Embracing the importance of resilience equips us with the ability to navigate challenges and setbacks, promoting personal growth and adaptability.

10. **Self-reflection:** Taking time for self-reflection allows us to gain clarity on our values, strengths, and areas for improvement, leading to a more fulfilling and intentional existence.

Benefits of embracing the paradigm shift.

1. Increased overall life satisfaction and fulfillment.
2. Greater clarity and direction in life, leading to better decision-making.
3. Enhanced mental and emotional well-being.
4. Stronger and more meaningful relationships.
5. Improved self-awareness and self-acceptance.
6. Heightened motivation and drive.
7. Increased resilience and ability to overcome obstacles.
8. Improved work-life balance and reduced stress.
9. Deeper sense of purpose and meaning in daily activities.
10. Enhanced personal growth and self-development.

Key qualities that support the paradigm shift.

1. Self-awareness.
2. Empathy.
3. Open-mindedness.
4. Compassion.
5. Authenticity.
6. Curiosity.
7. Flexibility.
8. Gratitude.
9. Patience.
10. Resilience.

Framework for embracing this paradigm shift

1. Assess your values and identify what truly matters to you.
2. Set clear goals and intentions aligned with your newfound understanding of importance.
3. Cultivate self-reflection practices such as journaling or meditation to deepen your self-awareness.
4. Prioritize self-care and create healthy habits that support your overall well-being.
5. Surround yourself with supportive and like-minded individuals who share similar values.
6. Practice gratitude daily by acknowledging the blessings and meaningful experiences in your life.
7. Engage in regular acts of kindness and contribute to causes that resonate with you.
8. Embrace challenges as opportunities for growth and view setbacks as learning experiences.
9. Seek opportunities for personal and professional development.
10. Regularly reassess and adjust your goals and priorities as you continue to evolve on your journey towards a meaningful existence.

Pros of embracing the paradigm shift.

1. **Sense of fulfillment:** Embracing a paradigm shift towards meaningful existence allows individuals to experience a deep sense of fulfillment and satisfaction in their lives.

2. **Enhanced well-being:** Focusing on the importance of one's actions and purpose in life can lead to improved mental and emotional well-being.

3. **Increased motivation:** When individuals recognize the significance of their actions, they are more likely to be motivated and driven towards achieving their goals.

4. **Higher resilience:** Embracing meaningful existence helps individuals develop higher resilience, enabling them to navigate challenges and setbacks with greater ease.

5. **Enhanced self-awareness:** This paradigm shift encourages individuals to reflect on their values, desires, and aspirations, leading to increased self-awareness and personal growth.

6. **Improved relationships:** When individuals prioritize meaningful existence, their relationships tend to strengthen as they align their values and goals with those around them.

7. **Greater productivity:** By focusing on the importance of their actions, individuals can enhance their productivity and efficiency, resulting in more meaningful and impactful outcomes.

8. **Sense of purpose:** Shifting towards meaningful existence provides individuals with a sense of purpose in life, giving them a reason to strive for greater things.

9. **Personal growth:** This paradigm shift facilitates personal growth as individuals actively seek opportunities for learning, development, and self-improvement.

10. **Contribution to society:** By embracing meaningful existence, individuals can actively contribute to society, making a positive difference in the lives of others.

Cons of embracing the paradigm shift.

1. **Ambiguity:** The pursuit of a meaningful existence can sometimes be ambiguous and subjective, making it challenging to define and measure.

2. **Pressure and stress:** The quest for meaning and significance can create pressure and stress, as individuals may constantly evaluate their actions in relation to their overall purpose.

3. **Time-consuming:** Embracing a paradigm shift towards meaningful existence requires time and effort, which can be a challenge in today's fast-paced and demanding world.

4. **Potential conflicts:** The pursuit of a meaningful existence may sometimes clash with societal or cultural expectations, leading to conflicts and difficult decisions.

5. **Uncertainty:** The search for meaning in one's existence may lead to uncertainty and confusion, as individuals question their beliefs, values, and life choices.

6. **Risk of self-absorption:** Focusing too much on personal meaning and purpose may inadvertently lead to self-absorption and neglect of others' needs and perspectives.

7. **Potential dissatisfaction:** If individuals are unable to align their actions with their desired meaning, they may experience feelings of dissatisfaction and frustration.

8. **Unrealistic expectations:** The pursuit of a meaningful existence may sometimes lead to unrealistic expectations, setting individuals up for disappointment if those expectations are not met.

9. **Social isolation:** As individuals prioritize their personal meaning and purpose, they may distance themselves from social activities and relationships that do not align with their values.

10. **Lack of external validation:** Embracing a paradigm shift towards meaningful existence often requires individuals to find validation from within themselves rather than relying on external recognition or achievements.

Advantages of embracing the paradigm shift.

1. Increased fulfillment and satisfaction in life.
2. Improved mental and emotional well-being.
3. Enhanced motivation and drive to achieve goals.
4. Development of resilience to overcome challenges.
5. Deepened self-awareness and personal growth.
6. Strengthened relationships based on shared values.
7. Enhanced productivity and efficiency.
8. Clear sense of purpose and direction in life.
9. Opportunities for continuous learning and self-improvement.
10. Positive contribution to society and making a difference.

Disadvantages of embracing the paradigm shift.

1. Subjectivity and ambiguity in defining and measuring meaning.
2. Pressure and stress associated with evaluating actions against overall purpose.

3. Time and effort required for embracing a meaningful existence.

4. Potential conflicts with societal or cultural expectations.

5. Uncertainty and confusion in the search for personal meaning.

6. Risk of self-absorption and neglecting others' needs.

7. Potential dissatisfaction if actions deviate from desired meaning.

8. Unrealistic expectations leading to potential disappointment.

9. Social isolation from activities and relationships that don't align.

10. Need for internal validation rather than relying on external recognition.

There Will Always be Another Storm.

A **Reflective Analysis.**

The statement "There will always be another storm" holds deep significance as it encapsulates the transient nature of life and the inevitability of challenges. Throughout history, humanity has experienced physical, emotional, and metaphorical storms in various forms. This essay aims to explore the multifaceted nature of storms, their impact on individuals and societies, and the valuable lessons we can learn from them. By examining historical events, literary works, and personal experiences, we will gain a comprehensive understanding of the enduring presence and significance of storms in our lives.

1. Physical Storms.

- **Natural Disasters:** Physical storms such as hurricanes, tornadoes, and earthquakes have always been a part of our planet's ecosystem. Their catastrophic impact on environments and communities is a testament to the immense power of nature.

- **Climate Change:** With the current global climate crisis, the frequency and intensity of storms are increasing. It highlights the urgent need to address and mitigate the adverse effects of human actions on our environment.

2. Emotional Storms.

- **Mental Health:** Like physical storms, individuals also face emotional storms within themselves. The pressures of modern life, personal challenges, and traumas can lead to emotional turmoil and psychological distress.
- **Coping Mechanisms:** Understanding emotional storms enables us to develop strategies and seek support systems to navigate through difficult times. Emphasizing self-care, therapy, and resilience can assist individuals in weathering emotional storms successfully.

3. Metaphorical Storms.

- **Social and Political Unrest:** Storms can manifest metaphorically as social and political upheavals. Revolutions, protests, and movements often resemble the turbulent nature of storms, representing the need for change and challenges to established power structures.
- **Economic Crisis:** Financial meltdowns, recessions, and economic downturns bear similarities to storms, disrupting stability and causing widespread turmoil. These events

highlight the interconnectedness of global economies and the need for adaptive strategies during periods of uncertainty.

4. Lessons from Storms.

- **Resilience:** Storms remind us of our innate capacity to rebuild and endure. Through tales of survival and examples from history, we can learn valuable lessons in resilience, adaptability, and the power of human spirit.

- **Preparedness:** Understanding the cyclical nature of storms urges us to be proactive in our preparations. By investing in disaster management systems, early warning mechanisms, and sustainable practices, we can reduce the impact of future storms.

- **Unity and Empathy:** Storms have a unique way of bringing people together, fostering solidarity and empathy. In times of crisis, individuals and communities tend to unite, demonstrating the importance of compassion and collective action.

Conclusion

1. "Victorious in the Storm" is not just a book; it is an experience. It is a journey that takes readers through the depths of despair and the heights of triumph, reminding us that the human spirit is capable of enduring and overcoming even the most tempestuous storms. With its masterful storytelling, compelling characters, and profound insights, this book stands as a testament to the power of resilience and the triumph of the human spirit. Prepare to be swept away by "Victorious in the Storm" and discover the immeasurable strength that lies within.

2. "Finding Forgiveness for Your History" encompasses the process of seeking and granting forgiveness for past actions and experiences. It involves self-reflection, self-acceptance, empathy towards others, seeking forgiveness from those affected, and letting go of resentment and anger. By engaging in this transformative journey, individuals can liberate themselves from the burdens of their history, experience personal growth, and create a more positive and fulfilling future.

3. Closing in on our objectives requires unwavering focus, determination, and a growth mindset. By understanding our objectives, embracing challenges, and adopting effective strategies,

we can overcome obstacles and steadily progress towards success. Remember, the journey may not always be easy, but the gratification lies in the effort, dedication, and resilience demonstrated along the way. So, close in on your objective, stay focused, and let your determination guide you to achieve remarkable accomplishments.

4. Knowing your goal is a fundamental aspect of personal growth and success. It provides clarity, focus, and direction, allowing you to make informed decisions and take purposeful actions. Having a goal fuels motivation, determination, and resilience, enabling you to overcome obstacles and achieve extraordinary results. Goals help you measure progress, track success, and make necessary adjustments along the way. They foster personal growth, align with your values and passions, and lead to a more fulfilling and meaningful life. Therefore, it is essential to invest time and effort in understanding your goals and working towards their realization. Embrace the power of knowing your goal, and unlock the potential to create the life you desire.

5. In ever-changing world, it is essential to actively strengthen our castle — our lives, relationships, careers, and overall well-being. By cultivating self-awareness, building strong foundations of physical and mental well-being, developing coping mechanisms, investing in relationships, and embracing change, we fortify our castle against the winds of adversity. As we embark on this journey of building resilience, let us remember that the process itself is transformative, enabling us to discover our true strength, wisdom, and the unwavering spirit that lies within. Strengthen your castle, and you will emerge as a resilient force, capable of weathering any story.

6. Strolling our thoughts is an essential aspect of personal growth, mental well-being, and overall life satisfaction. By harnessing the power of cognitive self-regulation, we can shape our thoughts, emotions, and behaviors in a way that serves our best interests. The benefits of thought control extend beyond the individual, positively impacting our relationships, achievements, and physical health. With mindfulness, cognitive restructuring, emotional regulation, and a supportive environment, we can take charge of our thoughts and create a more positive and fulfilling life. So, let us embrace this transformative practice and unlock the immense potential that lies within our minds. Remember, the power to control your thoughts ultimately leads to the power to control your life.

7. Recognizing and ending destructive patterns is an empowering journey towards personal growth and self-discovery. Through self-reflection, seeking support, and adopting healthier habits, individuals can break free from the detrimental impact of these patterns. While

challenging, the rewards of leaving behind destructive patterns are immeasurable, fostering a more fulfilling and positive life. By embracing change, individuals can create a new narrative, one characterized by resilience, self-compassion, and authentic personal growth.

8. The superhuman strength of optimism lies in its ability to empower, motivate, and transform individuals and communities. It provides numerous benefits such as improved mental and physical well-being, enhanced relationships, resilience, and success. However, it is essential to acknowledge and navigate the potential pitfalls associated with optimism, ensuring a balanced approach that integrates realism and critical thinking. By recognizing both the pros and cons, we can cultivate a resilient and constructive optimism that enables personal growth, fosters positive connections, and drives societal progress. Embracing the strength of optimism can help us navigate life's challenges with unwavering hope and inspire positive change in ourselves and the world around us.

9. The true power of collaboration lies in its ability to maximize individual potential, foster innovation, and drive positive change. This essay has shown that nobody can accomplish anything alone, highlighting the shared knowledge, strength in numbers, support, and motivation that arise from collaboration. It has also underlined the advantages of complementary skill sets, innovation, increased efficiency, and personal growth that are nurtured within collaborative environments. By recognizing and embracing the power of collaboration, individuals and society as a whole can

unlock their full potential and achieve greatness that would be unattainable through individual efforts alone.

10. Acknowledging the limitations of an achievement-driven mindset and embracing a shift towards prioritizing importance offers tremendous advantages - both personally and collectively. By recognizing the importance of self-reflection, cultivating meaningful relationships, and nurturing personal growth, individuals can lead more fulfilling lives. It is through this transformation that we can ultimately find lasting contentment, positively impact others, and contribute to a more empathetic and compassionate society.

11. The phrase "There will always be another storm" serves as a poignant reminder of life's inherent challenges. Whether in the form of physical, emotional, or metaphorical storms, their impact on individuals and societies is profound. By acknowledging and understanding the nature of storms, we can be better prepared to navigate them successfully, drawing upon the lessons of resilience, preparedness, and unity. Embracing the storms of life and learning from them ultimately strengthens our ability to weather future challenges and emerge stronger as individuals and as a society.

Afterword

As I reflect upon the journey we have undertaken within the pages of "Victorious in the Storm," I am filled with a mixture of emotions. The storm may have raged fiercely, testing the limits of our characters and challenging them in unimaginable ways, but through it all, they emerged victorious. Their triumph serves as a testament to the resilience of the human spirit and the power of hope.

In the aftermath of the storm, we find our characters forever changed. They have weathered the tempest, battled their inner demons, and emerged stronger, wiser, and more compassionate. The storms they faced were not merely external forces; they represented the trials and tribulations that we encounter in our own lives. Through their stories, we have gained insights, found solace, and discovered the strength to face our own storms head-on.

One of the most profound realizations we encounter in "Victorious in the Storm" is that storms, though initially daunting, can be catalysts for growth and transformation. They have the power to strip away our illusions, challenge our beliefs, and push us to our limits. It is within the crucible of the storm that we find the opportunity to redefine ourselves, to shed the old and embrace the new.

Our characters exemplify this transformative power. They have faced loss, heartbreak, and despair, yet they have refused to be defined by their circumstances. Instead, they have chosen to rise above the storm, drawing strength from within and finding the resilience to rebuild their lives. In their journey, we find inspiration to confront our own storms, to trust in our inner strength, and to believe that victory is possible, even in the face of seemingly insurmountable odds.

"Victorious in the Storm" also reminds us of the importance of community and connection. In times of struggle, it is often the support of loved ones, friends, and even strangers that carries us through. Our characters have been uplifted by the compassion, understanding, and encouragement of those around them. Their stories serve as a reminder that we are not alone in our storms, and that reaching out for help and offering support can make all the difference.

The storm, as a central metaphor in this book, represents not only the external challenges we face but also the storms within ourselves. It is a reminder that our own internal battles can be just as fierce and tumultuous as any external force. It is within the depths of these internal storms that we find our greatest opportunities for growth and self-discovery. By confronting our fears, embracing vulnerability, and embracing our authentic selves, we can emerge victorious, even in the face of the most daunting challenges.

In the aftermath of the storm, we are left with a sense of hope and renewal. The characters of "Victorious in the Storm" have shown us that no storm lasts forever, and that even the darkest clouds eventually give way to sunlight. They have taught us that victory is not measured by the absence of adversity, but by our ability to navigate through it with resilience, grace, and unwavering determination.

As we close the final chapter of "Victorious in the Storm," let us carry its lessons with us. Let us remember that storms, though tumultuous, are not insurmountable. They are opportunities for growth, catalysts for change, and reminders of our own inner strength. May we be inspired to face our storms head-on, to embrace the challenges that come our way, and to emerge victorious, knowing that we are capable of weathering any storm that life may bring.

I extend my heartfelt gratitude to the author for crafting such a powerful and thought-provoking narrative. Through their words, they have reminded us of the resilience of the human spirit, the transformative power of hope, and the importance of community. May "Victorious in the Storm" continue to inspire and uplift readers for generations to come, reminding us that no storm can extinguish the light that shines within us all.

In closing, may we carry the spirit of victory within us, knowing that we have the strength to overcome any storm that life may send our way. Let us embrace the challenges, learn from the hardships, and emerge stronger, wiser, and more compassionate. For it is in the storms of life that we find our true selves and discover the depth of our own power.

www.ingramcontent.com/pod-product-compliance
Lightning Source LLC
Chambersburg PA
CBHW070946260726
48661CB00003B/1141